THE MOSAIC MARRIAGE

HOW TWO IMPERFECT PEOPLE BECOME ONE MASTERPIECE

DR. TROY AND JANA JONES

Cover design by Christian Rafetto (www.humblebooksmedia.com)

Published in association with The Fedd Agency, Inc., a literary agency.

Fedd Books
P.O. Box 341973
Austin, TX 78734
www.thefeddagency.com

Paperback ISBN: 978-1-964508-32-0
Library of Congress Control Number: 2024924523

First Edition

Printed in the United States.

DEDICATION

To our two beautiful daughters,

Our love story wouldn't be complete without you. You are our joy, adding beauty and depth to our masterpiece. The men you married and our five precious grandchildren have only enriched our mosaic.

Now, it's your turn to create your own masterpieces. But never forget, it all began with a small-town girl and a city boy who deeply loved each other and were passionately devoted to Jesus together.

We Love You,
Dad & Mom

TABLE OF CONTENTS

Our Love Story

The atmosphere was electric, the air buzzing with excitement as the crowd of teenagers filled the room, their cheers echoing off the walls. I had someone build a chariot, a creation that looked straight out of a fairytale. Jana loves popcorn, so I had custom heart-shaped popcorn balls for everyone.

The kids were screaming as she was carried in on the chariot.

I got down on one knee and asked her to marry me. I fumbled for a second and realized I had misplaced the ring. Panic flashed through me, but I quickly found it, my heart pounding in my chest. When she said yes, the room erupted in cheers, sealing the memory as one of pure, chaotic, beautiful joy.

To truly understand our story, we've got to rewind. Let me take you back to where it all began.

Jana grew up in the small town of Kingston, Idaho—a close-knit community of fewer than 400 people. When she was just two years old, her parents divorced. Jana's mom remarried and experienced a radical transformation through her newfound faith. Her stepfather, who became her dad in every sense, made a profound and lasting impact on her life.

I come from a troubled home, filled with painful divorces, a dysfunctional family, and a broken home life. My early memories are of stepfathers belittling me and calling me a "bastard child" because I was born out of wedlock. Elementary teachers constantly confused my last name with one of my stepfathers, and I endured the embarrassment of stuttering, going in and out of speech classes through my elementary years. Amid this turmoil, a church community took me under their wing and paid for me to go to Bible camp. At 13, my life was radically transformed as I experienced the redeeming hope of the power of the gospel.

In January, 1988, our paths crossed in the most unexpected of places—a Bible Quiz match. I, a city boy from Renton, Washington, was the coach of the Renton team. She, a charming small town girl from Kingston, Idaho, was a quizzer on the opposing team, coached by none other than her own mom.

The match was intense, filled with high stakes and competitive spirit. During a critical moment, Jana buzzed in confidently, her voice steady and sure, and answered a question, securing 30 points for her team. I stood up, brimming with certainty, and contested her answer. She thought I was cocky. To her dismay, the judges agreed with my challenge, reversed her points, and ruled her answer incorrect. Her face tightened, her lips pressed together, and her eyes showed a flicker of frustration—a clear sign of her displeasure.

After the match, I introduced myself. But let's be real—I definitely wasn't scoring any points with her.

Her team made it to the final rounds. I found myself in the audience, watching her compete. That's when I noticed her in a different light. Amidst the competitive atmosphere, I saw not just an opponent but a strikingly beautiful girl. Her confidence and determination were captivating. Leaning over to my college buddy, I remarked, "Look at her. She's beautiful." Roger Archer chuckled and said, "That is my sister. Be careful."

Throughout the rest of the match, Roger kept nudging me, saying, "You two are perfect for each other. A match made in heaven." After the final buzzer sounded and the day came to a close, I mustered the courage to reintroduce myself to her. She was hesitant, and understandably so, but at least she knew my name.

Determined to win her over, I sent flowers to her school—a gesture that began to soften her heart.

One night, I shared my testimony with Jana, opening up about my faith. The moment was magical and authentic, sealing the connection between us. I fell in love with her and she with me.

The rest, as they say, is history.

Our long-distance relationship was fun. She wrote me a handwritten letter every day for over a year—388 letters in total. I received them in the mail every day, and two on Mondays. I drove five hours one way to Kingston, Idaho, 25 times in 18 months to see her. Let's just say I drove my car into the ground.

So, even though I misplaced the ring, she still said yes! That 'yes' sparked a love story that has since grown into one stunning masterpiece.

Nine months later, we got married on May 13, 1989. Jana was 19, and I was 22. We had absolutely no idea what marriage looked like or where to begin—just a small town girl and a city boy declaring to every married couple, "Don't stop believin'."

Looking back, we were a miracle in the making. All we had was innocent love and hearts surrendered to Jesus.

Our story is one filled with pain and hurt . . . we had to overcome generational patterns in our lives . . . but over the last 35 years God took two imperfect people and created ONE masterpiece.

So, take it from this city boy and small-town girl, and as Journey famously sang, 'Don't stop believin.'"[1] This anthem perfectly captures the heart of this book—especially if you can belt it out in the car without hitting any of the notes.

This book is 35 years in the making. Warning: it is filled with fun and intimate moments of our marriage. Some parts may even be PG-13. Read with caution. (PG, of course, standing for Praising God. Now this is perhaps the cheesiest thing I will say in this book.)

Let's do it!

WHAT'S AHEAD

Whether you've been married for fifty years, five years, five minutes, or you're not married yet, this book is for you. (And to all my single friends: you're in good company. Remember, two of the most influential figures in the New Testament—Jesus and Paul—were single.)

No matter the condition of your marriage, we wrote this book for you. Maybe your marriage is thriving, perhaps you're thinking about calling a divorce lawyer, or you're somewhere in between. It doesn't matter—this book is for you.

Maybe your spouse is "making you" read this book, or someone else is forcing it into your hands. I get it—some of the content might seem a little far-fetched. Maybe you're not a Christian, or maybe you've been hurt or betrayed, and you're thinking, "Can I really learn anything from this couple who doesn't know my circumstances?" Trust me, I've been there. It's like the first time I walked into a gym—I felt clumsy, out of place, and the whole thing seemed overwhelming. But I kept showing up (and still do). So here's my challenge to you: just show up and keep reading. If some of these ideas feel outdated or not your style, that's fine. But stick with it. Who knows, something might click—and it could be the unexpected breakthrough you didn't see coming!

Read each chapter asking God to do a miracle in your life. I almost called this book *Miracle on Your 34th Street*, but it didn't make the cut. Still, this small-town girl and city boy are believin' God for a miracle on your street.

So, grab your coffee, get comfy, and dive into these pages with an open heart and a bit of humor. After all, laughter is good medicine for the soul—and for a marriage.

Chapter 1: Clean Your Surface

The first step in creating any mosaic is to clean the surface. This means getting honest and removing the dirt and grime that has built up over time. Before any masterpiece can emerge, you must clean the surface daily. Your marriage will never be healthy if you carry around hurt, unmet expectations, bitterness, unforgiveness, disappointments, resentment, past traumas, and unresolved conflicts.

Chapter 2: Discover Your Mosaic

The second step is to discover the actual stones, tiles, and pieces of your mosaic—in other words, discover your spouse. Stop trying to change or fix them; instead, become wildly curious about who they are. Every tile in your mosaic is unique, and each piece is essential to the grand design. Your marriage has a color wheel with three primary and three secondary colors, creating an infinite spectrum of hues that make your relationship beautifully complex.

Chapter 3: Set the Tiles

The third step is to set the tiles. When setting the tiles of your mosaic, you must ensure they are safe and secure. We will explore how to have "Safe and Secure" conversations with your spouse. These conversations are meant to bond your hearts together, not tear them apart. For any mosaic to be a masterpiece, you must apply adhesive to the tiles to secure them firmly. This may be one of the most critical chapters of the book.

Chapter 4: Fill in the Gaps

The fourth step is to fill in the gaps. You will learn the importance of filling in the gaps of your marriage every day. Finish work is essential to the mosaic; it protects the edges and ensures no dirt and grime seep into the artwork.

Chapter 5: Polish Your Mosaic

The final step is to polish your mosaic. Here, we will discuss the role of sexual intimacy. Intimacy is the polish that brings your mosaic to life, adding a brilliant sheen that catches the eye and warms the heart. God created sex as an ongoing covenant renewal of your bond with each other. Learn how to polish your mosaic and restore the beauty of intimacy in your marriage.

Make sure you pay attention to the Couples Chat. These are open ended questions for you and your spouse to discuss. If you're engaged, these are fantastic questions to work through together. You might even consider finding a small group of others to participate in conversation over a seven-week period.

just jana
JJ

I pray for you as you read this book, whether you are single, single again, engaged, thinking about ending your marriage, or just trying to get better at loving each other. I pray for God's grace as you read on. I pray the power of the Spirit would touch each and every one of you. There are no easy answers, no one piece of advice that can resolve all the issues . . . but we serve a God who takes two imperfect people and turns them into ONE Masterpiece.

INTRODUCTION

Hello, my name's Troy, and I'm married to the love of my life, Jana. Our relationship isn't exactly stereotypical. I'm a man of many words, while she weighs hers carefully. Over the years, I've learned to listen more and talk less. A bit of warning: Jana may be a woman of few words, but when she speaks, her words are profound and deeply impactful.

Hi there, I'm Jana. Troy and I are excited to share with you the "secret sauce" of our marriage. We're praying it will be helpful to you. We love talking about the good, the bad, and the funny sides of every aspect of marriage. Our marriage didn't happen by accident; we've been intentional in every area. We've learned to be wildly curious about each other's differences. Keep an eye out for my icon, JJ (Just Jana), throughout the book for straightforward, no-nonsense insights. And who knows? You might even get a laugh or two along the way!

There is a prevailing narrative in our culture that 50% of marriages end in divorce, but this is simply not true. This misconception gained popularity in the early 1980s based on projection trends, not hard statistics. People accepted it as reality, but it is far from the truth. After an eight-year investigative study, social researcher and best-selling author Shaunti Feldhahn has demonstrated that the divorce rate has never reached 50%. In fact, it is significantly lower, currently closer to 30 to 40%, with only 20-25% of first marriages ending in divorce. And the divorce rate has actually decreased since 1980 (see appendix A for a summary of stats from Feldhahn).[2]

Mark Twain famously said, "There are three kinds of lies: lies, damned lies, and statistics." Lies are deceptive, but statistics can be even more dangerous. They often masquerade as truth, leading people down destructive paths. One of the most damaging statistics is the claim that 50% of marriages end in divorce. This grim figure has cast a long, dark shadow over marriage, eroding the hope of ever achieving a truly great one. For too long, we've allowed this bleak narrative to dominate our view of marriage.

But that ends now—today! It's time to rewrite the narrative about marriage. Let the world know that two people *can* become one masterpiece, no matter what anyone says or what life throws at them. Watch as God works a miracle in your marriage.

You can have an amazing marriage. Don't believe the lie of the culture. You don't have to live in some kind of unfounded fear or settle for a mundane, dry marriage. Your marriage is a masterpiece in the making!

The goal of this book is to inspire audacious hope for your marriage and change the marriage narrative in our world.

Yes, there are challenges, and trust me, we won't ignore these. But I want you to hear me say to you right now—no matter who you are or where you're at, your marriage can become a stunning masterpiece.

While these stats are encouraging, they are not something we should do handsprings about. It's like saying a plane has a 20%-30% chance of crashing—trust me, I wouldn't want to fly on that airline. While the numbers are better than we thought, the goal is not to avoid divorce, the goal is to have one of a kind, durable masterpiece.

THE DILEMMA

How can your marriage become a masterpiece instead of simply being mundane or at best, average? Why can marriage be so downright frustrating? Let's explore these questions together.

Imagine this: Two people meet and sparks fly. They fall head over heels, completely unaware of the countless variables they're dragging into their new relationship. Each one comes with a suitcase crammed full of unique stories, backgrounds, and narratives.

He's got a wild streak, molded by childhood summers spent conquering hiking trails with his family. She, on the other hand, treasures quiet moments, shaped by those cozy evenings spent reading with her grandmother. He dreams of launching a business empire, while she's passionate about molding young minds in the classroom. Their perspectives, goals, values, and family origins are as varied as the items in their suitcases.

And here's the kicker—he is a man and she is a woman. Despite what modern culture might preach, this alone marks a significant difference. You say tomato, I say tomahto. The differences are fun to laugh at but difficult to live with.

All these pieces are supposed to blend together into "ONE" as the minister says, "I now pronounce you husband and wife." But when the honeymoon is over (or even before it begins), you're left trying to figure out how to create the "happily ever after" marriage. Then, naturally, you want your partner to become like you—your personality, your stories, your traditions, your way of dealing with conflict, sex, and communication. Women marry thinking I can change him and men marry thinking I can change her. This is a recipe for disaster!

Then the minister says, "You may kiss your bride." And let's be honest, both are just hoping neither of you trips over the dress or faints from nerves at that point!

Read carefully this next line: the unique differences in your marriage can either create a durable, one-of-a-kind masterpiece or spiral into a chaotic, out-of-control disaster.

This is the heart of this book: I want to inspire audacious HOPE for your marriage. No matter where you are right now, no matter the struggles you've faced, I believe with all my heart that a thriving, fulfilling marriage is within your reach. Let this be the moment you embrace that hope and refuse to settle for anything less.

Your goal isn't to change or fix your spouse. Quite the opposite—I want you to be wildly curious about them. Get to know their quirks, dreams, and everything in between. Over time, as you blend all these pieces together, you'll create a new color palette—a stunning masterpiece that's uniquely yours.

Allow the differences in your marriage to be God's gift to you, or they will be the devil's playpen. Read this again! The enemy wants to destroy your marriage, and he will use your "differences" to ultimately ruin the beauty of your covenant. These differences can create beauty, texture, and depth in your marriage.

How do all these pieces come together? How do you create a mosaic marriage? You're reading the right book!

Instead of trying to keep up with the Joneses (pun intended), start creating a Mosaic Marriage. A Mosaic Marriage is a durable, one-of-a-kind masterpiece crafted from countless differences and even broken pieces. Like an artist uses small fragments of glass, stone, or tile to create a mosaic, you can use the unique and often broken pieces of your relationship to build something stunning.

Each piece, with its unique shape, color, and texture, contributes to the whole picture. And let's be honest, marriage doesn't come with an instruction manual—and even if it did, most men would probably glance at it, toss it aside, and say, "I've got this." But here's the beauty of it: sometimes those broken pieces make the most fascinating designs—turning what seems like a mess into a masterpiece. It's in the imperfect, the cracks, and the unexpected where the true art of marriage is formed, creating something more beautiful than we could have ever imagined.

It's not the "ideal" Cinderella and Prince Charming marriage. The problem with many marriage books and advice is that they often paint men and women with broad, stereotypical brushstrokes. Men want respect. Women want love. All true. Kind of. But it's more artistic than that. I'll do my best to discuss natural differences while recognizing that we are all unique and nuanced individuals, far more complex than the simple "stereotypes" suggest.

Our goal is for your marriage to be a Mosaic Marriage—durable, one of a kind! Like a piece of art, there is a story to be told and one to be celebrated. Our imperfections are not meant to be fixed or changed but embraced and celebrated as part of our unique marriage story.

This sounds all fancy and simple but way harder to do in everyday life. This may shock you, but just getting both people in a marriage to say out loud, "I am imperfect. I have weaknesses, nuances, quirks, and blind spots" may be the first step to God taking two imperfect people and turning them into ONE masterpiece.

just jana

I think we could all use a dose of humility. Humility is the glue that holds your marriage together. Say it out loud: "I am not perfect." Men, listen up: arrogance is not sexy. It's a major turn-off. Confidence, however, is a different story. Your wife wants you to be confident, not cocky. And ladies, let's not just point fingers at the men—we need to walk humbly before God and acknowledge our own weaknesses too. Remember, God hates pride because pride is the poison that seeps into every marriage. Humility is the glue that keeps it strong.

TWO BECOMING ONE

In Genesis, God declares, "the two shall become one flesh." This is not just poetic language; it's a divine blueprint for marriage. When God speaks of two becoming one, He's talking about more than just a physical union. He's describing a total integration of two lives—a blending so complete that what was once separate now exists as a singular, unified whole. It's like taking two distinct colors on a painter's palette and mixing them together. The result is something new, something richer, and something that neither color could be on its own—a stunning masterpiece!!

Timothy Keller captures the depth of marriage covenant when he says, "... a union between two people so profound that they virtually become a new, single person. This covenant brings every aspect of two persons' lives together. In love, they donate themselves, wholly, to the other."[3] Keller is right. This isn't just about sharing a home, a last name, or a bank account. It's about merging every part of your life—your dreams, your fears, your strengths, and your weaknesses—into one new color palette.

In marriage, you don't just agree to live with someone. You agree to die to yourself in ways you never imagined. You learn that love isn't about demanding your own way but about giving up your way for the sake of the other. And in that selfless abandonment, you find a deeper joy, a richer love, and a more profound sense of oneness than you ever thought possible.

Think about it: God designed marriage as the ultimate illustration of His relationship with us. Just as Christ gave Himself completely for the church, so we are called to give ourselves completely to our spouse. And in that giving, we discover the mystery and beauty of becoming one masterpiece—one in purpose, one in spirit, and yes, one in flesh. It's a holy and sacred bond, one that reflects the very heart of God's love for us.

So, when God says, "the two shall become one flesh," He's inviting us into something far greater than we can comprehend—a partnership that transcends the ordinary and touches the divine. It's a call to step into the fullness of what marriage was always meant to be: a living, breathing, tangible reflection of God's unbreakable covenant with His people.

The problem is most people think, "The two shall become me." The other person has to change and become like me. NO! The two shall become ONE masterpiece! This is the beauty of marriage.

Jana and I thought "becoming one" would be easy. We walked out of that little country church 35 years ago, hand in hand, convinced that "the two shall become one" would just naturally happen. Well, it turns out that's not how it works. It doesn't happen by accident—it requires intention, effort, and a lot of grace.

Jana and I see things differently, speak differently, and value different things. Sure, sex might be awesome, but it doesn't magically smooth over our differences. To make things even more complicated, I came from a broken home and had to confront some deep generational patterns. Honestly, I didn't really know what marriage was supposed to look like, let alone how to treat a lady!

So, why does "becoming one" feel like an impossible mission? Because we are different. If you had a front-row seat to our marriage, you'd see it. From a distance, you might see a stunning masterpiece, but up close? You'd know we're from two different planets!

- Jana is from a small town; I'm a city boy.

- Jana is an introvert; I'm an extrovert.

- Jana is an executor—she gets things done, no procrastination. Me? I write things down, make a to-do list, and *maybe* check it twice!

- Jana is practical and grounded; I'm big-picture and holistic.

- Jana is risk-averse; I am ok with the unknown.

- Jana is straightforward and no-nonsense; I enjoy conceptualizing ideas and plans.

- Jana recharges with quiet, reflective time; I get re-energized by going to a conference and being with life-giving people.

- Jana loves to deep clean; I prefer to organize (okay, maybe more like stack things somewhat neatly).

- Jana's love language is acts of service; mine is words of affirmation and physical touch.

- Jana reads the Bible devotionally; I read it theologically.

just jana *Yes, we are different. And trust me, we didn't make up this list just to make it look good in a book. After 35 years of marriage, I'm still shocked at how different we are! It still amazes me how we think, process, pray, problem-solve, and work in completely opposite ways. Honestly, sometimes I wonder if we're even on the same planet! But that's exactly what makes us a masterpiece. If you can figure out how to blend those differences—without wanting to strangle each other—you're well on your way to a stunning marriage. Stop fighting the contrast and start embracing it, because that's where the magic (and the fun) really happens!*

Now, some of you reading this might think, "Troy is a piece of work," while others might think, "Jana is a piece of work." And guess what? You're both 100% right—and 100% wrong. Together, we are a piece of art. We don't try to balance these differences; we blend them like colors on a palette to create something uniquely beautiful.

Yes, we're from two different planets. But over the past 35 years, we've learned how to blend our colors into a new, unified, and stunning masterpiece. Not perfect—it's got plenty of tiny fractures, but it's one that reflects honor and glory to our Master in heaven!

We can't wait to share this journey with you. We believe God can create a masterpiece in your marriage too. Buckle up—it's the holiest adventure of your life! Get ready for your marriage to become a canvas of God's honor and glory.

COUPLES CHAT

MARRIAGE EDITION

1. On a scale of 1-10 (1 being low, 10 being high), how much do you think the differences between you and your spouse have added depth and beauty to your marriage? Can you share a few examples where those differences have brought beauty to your relationship and others where they might have caused some frustration?

2. How do you and your spouse handle moments when one of you wants the other to be more like them?

3. In what ways have you intentionally worked to blend your unique backgrounds and stories into your mosaic?

4. What has been a significant turning point in your marriage where you realized the importance of appreciating each other's differences?

5. Have there been times when you or your spouse had to set boundaries to bring your true self into the relationship? How did that impact your marriage?

6. What steps have you taken to ensure that your marriage is a 'Mosaic Marriage'—durable and one of a kind?

7. What are your key goals in reading this book together? How can you ensure you get the most out of this experience, and what specific steps can you take to apply the lessons learned to your marriage?

ENGAGED EDITION

1. On a scale of 1-10 (1 being low, 10 being high), how comfortable are you with the differences between you and your partner? What are some specific differences that you believe could either strengthen or challenge your future marriage?

2. Take some time to share your personal story with your future spouse. Include as many details as possible—your childhood, key life experiences, and moments that have shaped who you are today.

3. Reflect on the meaning of the phrase "two shall become one" in the context of marriage. What does this concept mean to each of you as you prepare for your future together? How do you envision blending your lives, values, and goals to build a mosaic marriage?

4. Separately, take some time to list three desires you have for your future marriage. Once completed, come together and share them. Discuss what you've learned about each other.

5. What personal goals or dreams do you want to pursue within your marriage? How can you support each other's individual growth while still building a shared future?

6. How would you describe the balance of "giving" and "receiving" in your relationship? Do you feel that one of you gives more than the other, or is there an equal balance in your relationship?

7. As you prepare for marriage, what are your key goals for your relationship? How will you ensure that you stay intentional about creating a "Mosaic Marriage" rather than drifting into routine?

1

CLEAN YOUR SURFACE

Remove Dirt and Grime

WHEN BUILDING A MOSAIC MARRIAGE, you must regularly clean your surface. Just as an artist is meticulous about preparing a base and keeping it clean, you must have the same commitment to creating a lasting marriage. The surface you prepare and maintain will determine the strength and beauty of your mosaic.

When we talk about the surface, we're usually referring to what's on top—the part we can see, touch, and interact with. It's the visible layer, the obvious stuff anyone can spot.

But lean into this mosaic metaphor—the surface goes deeper. It's not just what's on the outside; it's what's hidden beneath the titles. It's the dirt and grime lodged under the roles we play. It's the stuff that doesn't show up right away but is there, silently eating away if we don't deal with it.

One of my main frustrations with marriage books and conferences is that they discuss issues like sexual intimacy, communication, and emotional needs without ever asking, 'How is the surface of your marriage?' You can learn all the communication skills in the world, but if your marriage is clouded with bitterness, hurt, and unresolved conflict, you will never create a stunning masterpiece.

Marriage problems stem from what you can't see, not what you can.

Bitterness and hidden pain impact everything in your marriage. Without ongoing cleaning of your surface and keeping it free from dirt and grime, your mosaic will never become a masterpiece. This is both a daily commitment and a lifetime process. I wish I could say it's a one-and-done deal, but life has a way of creating grime on our surface. It takes a lifetime of transparency with God, your spouse, and others to not only get your surface clean but, more importantly, to keep it clean.

In other words, the problem is NOT the problem. The problem is what lies beneath the mosaic and many times can't be seen by the eye.

If your marriage surface is full of dirt and grime, all the advice in the world will not help you create a masterpiece. And let's face it, all this dirt and grime ruin any romantic night! It's hard to set the mood when you're tripping over unresolved issues.

just jana

Your marriage will never be healthy if you're not healthy. It's easy to blame your spouse for the mess in your marriage, but you need to start with your own heart and surface. What's really going on inside you? If there's bitterness and pain in your heart, it's going to hurt your marriage—plain and simple. If you want a masterpiece, you've got to start by looking deep inside. Talk with a trusted friend, life coach, marriage mentor, or counselor to get to the root of what's really going on. And most importantly, talk to God. He's the one who can create a new spirit in you.

A CLEAN SURFACE

Ok, let's take a look at what a clean surface looks like. Warning: this next part of the book may be shocking to many of you. Brace yourselves, because what I'm about to share might seem like a bit of an old fashioned idealistic fantasy. In today's society, we're surrounded by models of dysfunction—think reality TV and social media drama. So, let this next part of the book rattle you a bit and wake you up. If you get these three elements at the very surface of your mosaic, EVERY other aspect of your mosaic will have strength.

1. Sacred Covenant

This covenant isn't just a promise between two people—it's a sacred vow made with God at the center. It's a commitment to love, honor, and cherish each other until death parts you. When you see marriage as this holy covenant, you're building something unbreakable, divinely designed to stand the test of time.

Picture this: you're standing at the altar on your wedding day, gazing into the eyes of your soon-to-be spouse. Many couples' vows, if they were honest, would sound something like this, "For better or for worse (as long as you keep getting better), in sickness, and in health (as long as it's not COVID-19), until death do us part (or until we can't stand each other anymore)."

While this may be honest, it's not a surface your mosaic can withstand. True covenant vows go beyond mere words—they are the bedrock of your Mosaic Marriage, far more enduring than any Hallmark card sentiment.

In Chapter 5, we'll explore how sexual intimacy serves as an ongoing covenant renewal—a tangible way to reaffirm your vows to your spouse. It's not just important; it's the very foundation upon which a beautiful mosaic is built.

Someone once asked Ruth Graham if she ever considered divorce with Billy Graham. She said, "Divorce, no. Murder, yes."[4] A sacred covenant says I am committed to you today, tomorrow, and forever—regardless of what you do. If you find yourself playing the divorce card during any conflict with your spouse the very surface of your mosaic is threatened.

Divorce should never be uttered or mentioned in your home. Period.

Let me pause here to speak directly to those of you who have been divorced. I come from a divorced home and understand the pain that accompanies it. Despite the brokenness you might feel, I truly believe in God's redemptive power to bring you a miracle of grace and hope for a future, whether married or single.

Your mosaic may seem shattered into countless little pieces, leaving you feeling hopeless. But there is hope for you. Today, I want to speak these words over you: The past is behind you. Put it under the blood of Jesus and trust God for your future.

I want you to embrace audacious hope while making an honest assessment. Don't gloss over the cracks—properly assess the condition of your heart's surface. Confront any lingering baggage head-on so you don't drag it into your future relationships. Believe wholeheartedly in the transformative power of God, knowing that He can take the shattered pieces and craft them into a stunning, new mosaic. Don't settle for anything less than a masterpiece.

2. Selfless Abandonment

Are you ready to die to yourself? Now that is a brutal way to start a section!

Your marriage surface requires a heart of humility and a mindset of servitude. When both partners embrace selfless abandonment, they create a marriage filled with honor and unconditional love.

This may surprise some well-meaning Christians, but the gospel is about dying to oneself. Marriage, in many ways, is God's chisel, sculpting us into the image of Christ. It's where we truly learn to give ourselves completely to another person. Ready for the Potter to refine you into the image and person of Jesus Christ?

> **JJ** **just jana**
>
> *I believe marriage is the Master Craftsman placing us on the wheel, shaping and molding us into the image of Jesus Christ. Just as the potter uses their hands and tools to refine the clay, God uses marriage to teach us what it truly means to walk like Jesus. Marriage teaches me to die to myself and serve another human being. This is why Troy and I serve each other. Now, I may not literally wash Troy's feet (though he might enjoy that spa treatment—despite his less-than-perfect toes), but I'm committed to serving him, just as he serves me. This is one of the divine purposes of the marriage covenant—it's about the Master Craftsman shaping us into the image of Christ.*

Consider this statement from Paul the Apostle: "Do nothing out of selfish ambition or vain conceit. Rather, in humility value others above yourselves" (Philippians 2:3-8). He anchors this in the life of Jesus, who, though God, made himself nothing and took on the nature of a servant.

Keller, in his writing on the 'meaning of marriage,' observes, "If two spouses each say, 'I'm going to treat my self-centeredness as the main problem in the marriage,' you have the prospect of a truly great marriage." [5]"This profound insight highlights essentials for a strong, fulfilling covenant: selfless abandonment, humility, and a willingness to defer to your partner's needs over your own." By committing to this level of self-examination and sacrificial love, couples can build a solid foundation for a lasting and God honoring masterpiece.

Keller also notes that "The essence of marriage is a sacrificial commitment to the good of the other. This means putting the needs and interests of your spouse above your own, creating a partnership based on selfless love and service."[6] By doing so, spouses help each other become the persons God designed them to be, fostering a deep, enduring covenant that stands the test of time.

A Scripture that has profoundly influenced my approach to conflict is 1 Corinthians 6:7: "The very fact that you have lawsuits among you means you have been completely defeated already. Why not rather be wronged? Why not rather be cheated?" This verse challenges the very core of our pride, doesn't it? It's a call to lay down our need to be right, to win every argument, and instead choose peace over being proven correct. Imagine what would happen in our marriages if we lived this out—letting go of petty battles, embracing humility, and allowing love to cover those offenses. Sometimes, the real victory is in surrendering the fight.

You need to abandon your right to be right. It's shocking how many spouses prioritize being right over nurturing a healthy relationship. Right is overrated! What matters more is crucifying your flesh and fostering unity.

How can two people become one masterpiece if they're always fighting to be right, always clinging to their own agendas? Selfishness is like a stubborn stain on the surface of your mosaic. To create something beautiful, you must be willing to let go of your individual desires and build a masterpiece together.

Imagine if we all adopted that mindset in our marriages. Besides, being right all the time sounds exhausting . . . and frankly, kind of boring. I'd much rather have harmony with Jana than the discord of trying to win every argument.

3. Shared Submission

There's a dangerous misnomer out there that marriage is 50/50. I couldn't disagree more. Marriage is 100/100—sometimes even more. It's two people going all-in, fully submitted to each other. It's the blending of two lives, fiercely committed to Shared Submission. And that's the start of your marriage becoming a masterpiece. When you're both 100% in, that's when the real beauty begins to take shape.

Okay, I said it. The old-fashioned word: submission. Should wives submit to their husbands? Yes. Okay, I know I just lost at least 50% of my audience. "This guy is so old-fashioned. I feel sorry for his wife." But stay with me. Should husbands submit to their wives? Absolutely yes! And there goes the other 50%. But I may have gained back a few of the ladies.

When we think of the word "submission," it's easy to imagine something negative or oppressive. However, in the context of a Christian marriage, submission is a beautiful act of love and service.

Shared Submission is beautifully illustrated by harmony in an orchestra . . . sometimes the trumpet needs to sound louder than the violin, other times the violins need to take the lead, and occasionally, the drums need to set the pace. The pieces of an orchestra mutually defer to each other. When both partners are committed to submitting to each other, it becomes less about who's right and more about what's best for the relationship.

Shared Submission involves two people deferring to each other. The word "deferring" means to yield or submit to the opinion, decision, or judgment of another person.[7] When you defer to someone, you let them take the lead or make the final decision, often out of respect for their expertise, authority, or preference.

Deferring to one another is not about dominance or control, but about mutual respect and honor. When you practice shared submission, you acknowledge each other's strengths and weaknesses, working together to create a masterpiece of God's grace. This means both partners are willing to put their egos aside and listen to each other. It's not about one person always getting their way, but about both people valuing each other's perspectives.

Marriage is a race to serve and defer to each other. Imagine a couple arguing over who gets to do the dishes because they both want to give the other a break. Picture them bickering, not about who's right, but about who gets to pamper the other more. They're in a constant tug-of-war of kindness, each one fighting to let the other go first. Now that's the kind of battle worth having, right?

When a married couple comes to me with a problem, one of the first questions I ask is: "Have you totally, without hesitation, submitted to one another? Really?" I look at the lady and say, "Are you submitted to him? His needs, desires, thoughts, and dreams?" Then I look at the man and say, "Are you submitted to her? 100%. Her emotions, desires, dreams, insecurities, expectations?"

Often, the only Scripture men have memorized is Ephesians 5:22, "Wives, submit yourselves to your own husbands." Men, back up one verse and read this in total context, "Submit to one another out of reverence for Christ" (Ephesians 5:21). We are called to submit to one another out of respect for Christ. Paul reminds the ladies specifically to submit to their husbands. But then he boldly reminds men, "Husbands, love your wives, just as Christ loved the church and gave himself up for her." (Ephesians 5:25) Men, we are called to be willing to die for our spouse, not to get our own way or argue over trivial matters.

Men, a little tip: There is not a lady on this planet that won't willingly submit to you if you love your wife just as Christ loves the church. Love her sacrificially, and she'll be your biggest fan. Ladies, while our men are supposed to be like Christ, let's be honest—they are not Christ. They won't get it perfect. You don't get it perfect either. So, give him some grace, laugh when things are a little wonky, and still, submit to him out of reverence for Christ.

There's an old saying, "The man is the head, but the woman is the neck, and she can turn the head any way she wants." To me, this seems like a demeaning way to refer to the covenant relationship. I prefer to think of my wife as the crown. A wise proverb says, "A wife of noble character is her husband's crown" (Proverbs 12:4). A crown is worn as a symbol of authority, power, legitimacy and beauty. Instead of the neck analogy, I prefer saying, "The man is the head, but the woman is the crown, and she adds beauty to the entire home." Maybe we need a Hallmark movie called "The Crown of Christmas," featuring your spouse. Plus, it sounds way more romantic and less like a chiropractor's advertisement. Together, you create a royal partnership where each act of selflessness and love adds to the beauty of your shared life.

Alright, confession time: Shared Submission is easy to explain but tough to do. Take driving, for example. Jana struggles with Shared Submission when I'm behind the wheel. She likes to offer her directions—watch for this car, turn here, slow down there. Wisdom says it's time for me to stop writing and let Jana pop in and give her side.

JJ just jana

Troy is a safe driver. The problem is he likes to talk when he drives. And I'm not exaggerating when I say he'd rather talk than drive. I know some of you women think this is awesome—constant conversation, right? But he goes in the slow lane . . . drives me crazy. He will literally miss an exit because he's so busy talking. If I try to remind him, it's like I've interrupted his entire world. Yes, I need to submit. But seriously, Troy . . . could you just pay attention to the exit once in a while? It's like playing a game of 'Guess the Destination' every time we get in the car!

Alrighty, back to the book.

Let's face it, there will be times of real, gut-wrenching disagreements and even millions of small ones. How does Shared Submission work when there's a major disagreement? What happens when you are not sure what instrument in the orchestra should be louder? Who gets to decide?

After our first two girls, Jana and I hit one of those times. I wanted a third child; she did not! How do you submit to each other when you disagree on something this personal? It's not easy, and the answer isn't straightforward. In Chapter 3, "Set the Tiles," I untangle this complex web. Trust me, you won't want to miss this!

HOW TO CLEAN THE SURFACE OF YOUR MARRIAGE

Cleaning the surface of your marriage is a must if you want to create a masterpiece. It's time to get real and raw, scrubbing away the dirt and grime that poison the very surface of your heart. This isn't just spring cleaning; it's a soul-deep purification.

I wish I could say this is a once-and-done process. The truth is, cleaning the surface of your marriage is a daily commitment. Life happens. Mistakes happen. Every day, Jana and I make it a point to clean the surface of our hearts.

Here are some tried and true methods to keep the surface of your marriage clean.

1. Don't keep records of wrongs

Keeping a tally of every mistake is a surefire way to build up resentment. Scripture is very clear on the definition of covenant love: love keeps no record of wrongs (1 Corinthians 13:5). Instead of holding onto grudges, let things go. Your marriage isn't a courtroom, and you're not the judge. Forgive! Don't hold this against your spouse—just move forward.

Imagine trying to create a masterpiece with broken pieces that don't fit because of past offenses. Keeping score in marriage turns your relationship into a battleground where each mistake is ammunition for the next conflict. Instead, let love be the glue that holds your mosaic together, allowing each piece to fit without the burden of past hurts.

Holding onto wrongs is like drinking poison and expecting the other person to suffer. It's toxic. Ephesians 4:31-32 advises us to "get rid of all bitterness, rage, and anger, brawling and slander, along with every form of malice. Be kind and compassionate to one another, forgiving each other, just as in Christ God forgave you." Let go of the poison and embrace the freedom that comes with forgiveness.

Here's the truth: Quickly forgiving your spouse is the key to a strong, loving relationship. Ruth Graham nailed it when she said, "A happy marriage is the union of two good forgivers."[8] Forgiveness isn't optional; it's essential. Holding onto grudges or harboring resentment will only create division and bitterness.

No matter what your spouse has done, bitterness will destroy the beauty of your mosaic. Forgive your spouse.

just jana JJ *Instead of keeping a mental list of every little thing your spouse has done wrong, imagine a chalkboard that you wipe clean every night. Take out your eraser and clear that board. Every night before I go to bed, I say, "Tomorrow is a new day." Let tomorrow be a fresh start—not a rerun of past grievances and old arguments. Your marriage deserves the fresh start that forgiveness brings each and every day. Picture picking up that eraser . . . now stand at the chalkboard and erase until you can't even see a hint of that white dust. This makes things easier to wake up with a fresh start.*

2. Stay Pure

Purity isn't just about physical faithfulness; it's about emotional and mental integrity too. Guard your thoughts and your heart. Be transparent with your spouse. Flirting with someone else, even just emotionally, is like playing with fire—someone's bound to get burned.

Purity is about more than just staying faithful in body. It's about safeguarding your mind and emotions. It means setting boundaries, being honest about your feelings, and not giving any part of yourself to someone else that belongs to your spouse. It's about keeping your marriage bed—and your heart—pure.

Sexual intimacy is a vital part of a pure marriage. It strengthens the bond between you and helps keep your hearts connected. Don't underestimate the power of physical intimacy in maintaining emotional and mental purity. In Chapter 5, we will dive into the importance of intimacy in your mosaic and discuss why we should never allow a rattlesnake into our bedroom.

> **JJ just jana** *Purity is both an individual responsibility and a couple's mandate. Troy and I take this seriously in our marriage. We both have to keep our hearts and eyes clean while fostering a healthy intimacy together. My guess is some of you have already skipped ahead to Chapter 5 on sexual intimacy. But if you haven't, don't miss it. It's steamy and hot. And yes, it's as hot as it sounds—no, I'm not just talking about Troy's writing.*

3. Don't Go to Bed Angry

Jana and I never go to bed angry. We take Paul's advice literally: "Do not let the sun go down while you are still angry" (Ephesians 4:26). This may be some of the most practical advice to keep your surface clean. Anger can become a silent destroyer of marriages. It's like hidden mold that slowly spreads and weakens the foundation of your mosaic. This mold, if left undealt with, can be toxic to the marriage.

Mold often produces a musty, unpleasant smell that can permeate your home and be difficult to remove. This odor can make living spaces uncomfortable and unwelcoming. In the same way, undealt with anger or hurt can create an atmosphere of tension and discomfort in your marriage.

I know some of you are thinking, "This means we will have some long nights." Well, yes, it might. Long nights and groggy mornings are better than a moldy surface. Trust me, you don't want to wake up next to a relationship that's rotting from the inside out.

So next time you're tempted to hit the pillow still fuming, remember: better a little lost sleep than waking up to the stench of unresolved anger.

4. Own It and Apologize

We all mess up. When you do, own it. Owning it and, if necessary, apologize if you hurt your spouse in any way. Owning something and apologizing are two different things. You can own an action without apologizing, but you can't apologize without owning it. Let me explain.

If you were able to peek into a 24-hour day with Jana and me, you would hear words like this all the time: "This is on me." "My bad." "I missed this." "I should have communicated better on this." From time to time, you will also hear us say, "I am sorry I hurt you." We apologize when we hurt each other; we own it in everyday life.

When apologizing, say "I'm sorry" and mean it. No excuses, just a heartfelt apology. A simple, sincere apology can go far in healing wounds and building trust.

HOW IS YOUR SURFACE?

Our home was built in 1896, and let me tell you, it's got stories to tell. You'll hear more about that in the chapters ahead.

If you walked into my house, you'd probably marvel at the high ceilings, soak in the rich history woven into every nook and cranny, admire the perfectly chosen color palette, the furniture that feels like it was made just for this space, the seamless flow of the layout, or maybe even the cozy backyard with its inviting deck and beautiful landscape. But I doubt anyone would ask, "So, how's your foundation?"

And yet, that's the real question, isn't it? Because if your foundation—the surface, in this analogy—is compromised, the entire house is at risk.

A few years ago, we had a rat problem in our foundation. These weren't your garden-variety mice; these were big, bold, field rats, and they were relentless. The smell—imagine rotten potatoes mixed with something far worse—kept creeping into our home. We tried small mouse traps, thinking we could handle it, but those little guys had already set up shop. They were nesting in our insulation, shredding it to bits, and one particularly adventurous rat tried to come up through a pipe in our pantry. It got stuck, died, and started to decay. The stench was unbearable.

We called in a rat specialist, who confirmed our worst fears: the rats had wreaked havoc under our home. We had to rip out and replace the entire crawl space insulation and clean out the rat urine and feces. Thousands of dollars later, we had a brand new crawl space. And now, we have a pest control service that regularly checks our home to make sure it doesn't happen again—because let's be honest, nobody wants uninvited guests, especially the four-legged kind.

So, how's the surface of your marriage? What kind of "rats" are causing you problems? Is it time to hire some pest control for your relationship? Is there any mold growing in the basement of your heart? How's your Sacred Covenant? Are you honoring that holy commitment daily? How's the Selfless Abandonment? Are you dying to yourself each day? And what about your Shared Submission? Are you mutually putting each other's needs above your own? If any of these areas are weak, it's like having rats in your foundation—or worse, mold growing unseen. It's time to clean it up.

Some of you might feel like your surface is beyond repair. But don't stop believin'. There is hope! It can seem overwhelming to know where to begin the healing process. But just as a mosaic artist carefully restores each tile to create a masterpiece, you too can start to mend your marriage. In Appendix B, we provide "Seven Steps to Repair a Broken Marriage." Please read this and let it be a guide to your mosaic miracle.

So, I know this might seem like a strange question to start a marriage book with, but it's the most important question of this book: how's the surface of your marriage doing? If you don't get this right, the rest of the book is just a waste of your time.

Keeping your surface clean is not glamorous, but necessary. Roll up your sleeves, get to work, and watch your marriage transform into the masterpiece God intended.

At the risk of standing on my soapbox, let me say it one more time—the problems in your marriage have nothing to do with what you see; they have everything to do with what you can't see. The problem is NOT the problem. The real issue lies beneath the mosaic tiles—a lack of Sacred Covenant, Selfless Abandonment, and Shared Submission.

Think of it like an iceberg; it's not the tip above the water that sinks the ship, but the massive chunk lurking below.

Pro Tip for Wives:

just jana *Seven Ways to Pray for your man*

Alright, ladies, this one's just for you. Don't worry, men—I won't leave you hanging. I've got a handful of pro tips sprinkled throughout the book just for you, too.

1. A Prayer for His Relationship with God

   "Lord, I pray that my husband will grow closer to You every day. May he seek You with all his heart, find joy in Your presence, and trust in Your plans for his life. Strengthen his faith and help him to walk in Your wisdom and truth."

2. A Prayer for His Health and Well-being

   "Heavenly Father, I pray for my husband's physical, emotional, and mental health. Grant him strength and healing, protect him from harm, and fill him with peace and energy. Help him to take care of his body, mind, and soul as Your temple."

3. A Prayer for His Work and Purpose

   "Lord, I ask for Your blessing over my husband's work. Give him wisdom, creativity, and perseverance in all he does. Help him to work with integrity and excellence, knowing that he serves You in everything he undertakes."

4. A Prayer for His Protection

   "Father, I pray that You will protect my husband from any harm, danger, and negative influences. Guard his heart and mind, and keep him safe from physical and spiritual attacks. Surround him with Your angels and let him feel Your presence."

5. A Prayer for His Leadership

   "God, I pray for my husband as the leader of our home. Give him a heart that seeks Your guidance and follows Your direction. Help him to lead with humility, love, and grace, reflecting Your character in all he does."

6. A Prayer for His Friendships and Community

   "Lord, I pray that You surround my husband with godly friends and mentors who encourage, challenge, and support him. Help him to build deep, meaningful relationships that strengthen his walk with You and enrich his life."

7. A Prayer for His Love and Commitment to Our Marriage

   "Dear God, I pray for our marriage and ask that You strengthen the bond between us. Help my husband to love me as Christ loves the Church, with patience, kindness, and selflessness. May we grow closer to each other and to You every day."

COUPLES CHAT

MARRIAGE EDITION

1. On a scale of 1-10 (1 being dirty, 10 being clean), how would you rate the surface of your marriage right now? What are some things that might be slowly causing dirt and grime to build up on that surface?

2. What does the concept of a "Sacred Covenant" mean to you? How has viewing your marriage as a covenant changed the way you approach challenges in your relationship?

3. In what areas of your marriage do you struggle with selflessness? How can you practice "Selfless Abandonment" to better serve your spouse's needs?

4. What are some practical ways you can practice "Shared Submission" in your daily interactions? How can you better listen to and respect each other's perspectives and decisions?

5. Reflect on a time when you held onto a past hurt or grudge in your marriage. How did it affect your relationship? What steps can you take to let go of past wrongs and prevent them from clouding your surface?

6. How do you ensure that your marriage remains pure, both emotionally and physically? Are there any boundaries or practices you need to put in place to protect the purity of your relationship?

7. What is one habit you can commit to as a couple to keep the surface of your marriage clean? How can you hold each other accountable to regularly practice this habit?

ENGAGED EDITION

1. On a scale of 1-10, how prepared do you feel for the transition from engagement to marriage? What are the areas where you both feel confident, and what areas feel a little unsteady?

2. How do you define the "us" in your relationship? What are the shared values, habits, or goals that you both bring into the marriage?

3. What role will your families play in your marriage? Have you discussed the expectations, boundaries, and involvement of your parents and extended family?

4. What does the concept of a "Sacred Covenant" mean to both of you? How does viewing your marriage as a covenant, not just a contract, change the way you approach commitment, forgiveness, and challenges?

5. What does it mean to you to "die to yourself" in the context of marriage? Are there specific areas where you foresee the need to let go of personal desires or preferences?

6. How do you feel about the idea of Shared Submission in your relationship? What does mutual submission look like for both of you in terms of making decisions and honoring each other's needs?

7. What are your long-term dreams as a couple? Have you taken the time to discuss career goals, starting a family, and how you plan to pursue those dreams together while supporting each other?

2

DISCOVER YOUR MOSAIC

Be Wildly Curious About Your Spouse

SEVEN YEARS INTO OUR MARRIAGE, Jana and I had a wake-up call. It was one of those defining moments that shakes you to your core and makes you face who you really are. Looking back, we both agree that it changed us forever, molding us into the people we are today.

As a young family with two little ones—Kaylee, three, and Chelsey, one—we were living in a church parsonage built back in 1896. (And yes, I can still smell the aged wood like it was yesterday.) The character of that old house completely stole our hearts. It became the home I never had growing up. To say it was sentimental to me is an understatement. Then came the news—the church decided it was time to tear it down to make way for our new church building.

One night while playing Monopoly, I said out loud, "I want to save this house." My friend, always up for a challenge, dared me to move it. In a moment of sheer brilliance (or insanity), I decided, "Let's move it." Yes, you read that right. Why not move a house with two small kids?

Jana knew I had this idea, but let's just say my communication skills were lacking. The day the contractors showed up—I forgot to mention the exact time. She was up early with our two little girls when, suddenly, the contractors arrived and started digging around the foundation. The entire house shook like we were in the middle of an earthquake.

One week later, the big move happened.

The house creaked and groaned as it inched down the highway, suspended high above the road on a slow-moving convoy. Traffic snarled to a standstill, and the golfers, trapped in their cars, fumed as their tee times slipped away, while Maple Valley Highway turned into an unexpected parade route. Two miles later, the house settled on blocks at its new location. Workers swarmed, tools in hand, ready to stitch it back together, piece by piece.

Let's just say, Jana was *not* amused.

Then I came up with another idea to save money. "Let's move back into the house while they do the work," I said, thinking I was brilliant. "Save money." My wife had two babies and no kitchen. She almost had a nervous breakdown by the time the home was finished. I am sure I was not going to win the Husband of the Year award.

just jana

I was shocked. Here I am feeding my two babies, and I hear heavy equipment digging around the house. It was the contractors who were getting ready to move the house. I thought we were just playing our regular Monopoly, not a real-life "House Movers Edition."

After the kitchen was finished, she had it. She was venting and sharing her emotions, and I, in my infinite wisdom, said, "Look at these cabinets . . . I made them for you." Although, let's be real, I couldn't swing a hammer if you paid me.

She burst out in tears. "You don't love me." "You don't care for me." "You don't . . ."

I was deeply confused and utterly shocked, and an inward irritation started to build up faster than a pressure cooker.

In that moment, I saw the exasperation and sadness in her eyes, the way her shoulders slumped, and her voice quivered with each word. It was a wake-up call. The look in my wife's eyes and the realization that my efforts were not meeting her needs hit me like a ton of bricks. I realized I needed to figure out how to be married. How to serve my wife. How to be the man that no one ever modeled for me. How to break generational patterns over my life. That day, it wasn't just the house that needed to be moved and rebuilt—it was me. Who knew a game of Monopoly could lead to a marriage moment that would last forever?

JJ just jana *This moment wasn't just a turning point; it was a full-on, life-altering revelation. I hit rock bottom. I had a nervous breakdown. For years, I only knew how to say yes and please everyone around me. The hardest lesson I had to learn was setting boundaries—not just in our marriage, but in every facet of my life. It was tough. I had to stop being a doormat and start being a partner. It wasn't just about supporting Troy—it was about bringing my true self into the relationship and celebrating the masterpiece we were creating together.*

As the tension in our home reached a breaking point, I knew I had to step up and make some of the biggest decisions of my life. For the next 12 months, I was completely consumed with understanding Jana and learning how to be a husband who honored God and served my wife.

I interviewed couples who had been married a lifetime and were still happy (they do exist!), read every marriage book I could find (yes, even the ones with cheesy titles), talked to a counselor, and did everything possible to learn. I know some of you are wondering about podcasts. Remember, this was 1996. I would have had to get into a DeLorean and travel to the future to hear those. Well, people tell me I look like Michael J. Fox; perhaps I should have. Sorry, I got distracted for a moment.

Your mission is to discover your spouse. You're not tasked with understanding all men or all women—thankfully, because it would be easier to solve a Rubik's Cube blindfolded. Sure, we'll unpack the differences between men and women in the next section, but don't get lost in the details. Your focus is clear: be curious about your spouse. The only uncharted territory you need to explore is the person you married. Your goal? Simple: figure out who this person you married actually is. Learn them, truly know them, and before you know it, you'll have a marriage that's a masterpiece.

Here is the irony: you will never completely figure out your spouse. And just when you think you have, they'll change and morph. Life will happen. Kids will come. Jobs will change. Society will shift. All of this will change both of you. Your spouse is a mystery, with layers upon layers waiting to be uncovered. That's the wonder of marriage! You'll never fully understand them, and that's perfectly fine.

So, what's your job? To stay wildly curious about them and never stop believin'. Your spouse has untold layers and a rhythm all their own, just waiting to be discovered.

Does this mean you need to accept abusive behavior from your spouse? Absolutely not. I'm not talking about tolerating sexual affairs, physical harm, or controlling behavior—those are non-negotiable. What I'm talking about are the millions of everyday quirks and nuances of your spouse that you need to approach with wild curiosity. Those little things that make them who they are—those are worth exploring, not fixing.

Your "Mosaic" is one of a kind, a beautiful blend of unique pieces that come together to form a masterpiece. Just like the tiles in a mosaic, each piece of your marriage—every quirk, strength, and even flaw— adds to its beauty and resilience. It's the differences, the jagged edges, and the unexpected colors that make it truly remarkable.

just jana

JJ *Before we move on, you need to hear the rest of the story about that old house we moved down the street early in our marriage. Thirty years later, we're still living in it! That place sparked a deep love in Troy's heart for old homes. (Mine too, but shhh . . . don't tell him. If he knew how much I loved it, we'd probably be moving another one by next week!) We raised our girls here, one of our daughters was even married in the backyard during the 2020 pandemic, and now our grandbabies sleep in the same rooms our girls once did. I know, we're not supposed to get all sentimental about a house, but here's the truth—this isn't just a house. It's our home. And if we ever moved? The whole family would probably revolt! There's just too much history here—the scraped knees on the front steps, the late-night talks in the living room, the celebrations, the tears, the prayers. This house isn't just four walls; it's woven into the very fabric of our family's story. I'm pretty sure Troy would sooner sell a kidney than ever put a "For Sale" sign out front!*

Wild curiosity is like imagining standing on the edge of the Grand Canyon for the first time, feeling awestruck by its grandeur and the layers of rock telling their ancient stories. That's the kind of awe I want you to feel when you look at your spouse. Let them stir a wild curiosity within you. See the depth, the beauty, and the colorful details that make up who they are, and watch as these pieces come together to create the marriage masterpiece you craft together.

It's this curiosity—this desire to uncover every unique tile in your spouse's mosaic—that transforms a marriage from mundane to magnificent, turning it into a one-of-a-kind masterpiece.

THE MARRIAGE COLOR WHEEL

The foundational step to becoming wildly curious about your spouse is what I call your Marriage Color Wheel. It's about coming to the place where you not only celebrate your differences but grab the paintbrush of marriage and, with excitement, add color to every aspect of your life together. Some of your marriages are colorless because you want your spouse to mimic your color. Don't. Let both colors shine brightly. Blend them together. Create your own marriage color palette.

These primary colors, secondary colors, and the different hues create an infinite array of colors you create together. This vibrant and dynamic palette should make you wildly curious about the one you said "I do" to. Dive into the depths of each hue, celebrate the spectrum, and paint a durable, one of a kind masterpiece of a marriage.

There are three primary colors are—Red, Yellow, and Blue (RYB). When you blend these primary colors, you create three secondary colors: Green, Orange, and Purple.

These six colors are only the beginning point of your mosaic. Together, you can create an infinite array of hues that form your unique color palette. Each color and hue represents a fundamental aspect of your mosaic.

Primary Colors

1. Red | Passion and Sexual Intimacy

2. Yellow | Warmth and Communication

3. Blue | Calm and Emotional Connection

For a summary of the six colors in the Marriage Color Wheel, see Appendix B. In this chapter, I will focus on the three primary colors of your mosaic. We'll paint some secondary colors as we continue to build your mosaic in the following chapters.

Every other color on earth contains one of these primary colors. There are millions of hues and colors that make up the fabric of your marriage. No two marriages have the same color blends. It's beautiful. It's colorful. And just like the Grand Canyon changes colors with the seasons and years, with wild curiosity and creativity, you can transform your marriage into a vibrant, colorful masterpiece.

Red | Passion and Sexual Intimacy

Early in our marriage, someone shared a quirky piece of advice that caught our attention: "If you put a jellybean in a jar every time you have sex during the first year of your marriage and then remove one every time afterward, you'll never empty the jar." Well, being young, curious, and maybe a little competitive, Jana and I decided to test the theory. We got a jar and stocked up on jellybeans.

But we didn't stop there. In true Troy-and-Jana fashion, we gave each color a meaning. Red jellybeans were our favorite—they represented the "hot" nights. Let's just say red quickly became the MVP of the jar.

The experiment was fun—a little inside joke that added some spice and laughter to our early years. Unfortunately, somewhere along the way—during our first move—the jar disappeared. Poof. Gone. We never did find out if the theory was true.

But here's what I can say with confidence: the jar might have vanished, but we didn't let the red jellybeans disappear from our marriage. Keeping the "red" alive has been one of the most intentional and rewarding commitments we've made. It's not just about sex; it's about passion, connection, and prioritizing each other—even when life gets busy, chaotic, and downright exhausting.

So, no, the jellybean theory didn't hold up. But the lesson did: don't let your jar go empty. And whatever you do, keep those red jellybeans in the mix.

Red, the color of passion and intimacy, symbolizes a hue that adds beauty to every marriage. It embodies desire, excitement, and deep connection. You must become wildly curious about the red in your spouse. Sexual intimacy means recognizing the importance of physical touch and intimacy, which fuels passion and strengthens the bond between partners.

To state the obvious: God has wired us differently with unique sexual drives. Men tend to sprint toward sex, while women may take a more leisurely walk toward it, but both deeply desire intimacy. Both have different hues of red.

Ladies, why does a man's sexual desire ignite like a sprinter at the starting line, muscles tensed, heart racing, ready to explode with energy at the starter's gun? Discover the reason behind this. Never lose your curiosity. Don't just say this is how men are. God created your man like this.

Men, why do women prepare for intimacy like running a 5K, stretching slowly, finding their rhythm, each step deliberate as they gradually warm up? Why does it seem their hues of intimacy are different from ours? God created your wives red like this for a reason. I believe it is teaching men that sex is more than physical but also emotional intimacy. Never get tired of those questions. Be curious about your wife's red! Learn your spouse.

Sometimes women get a bad rap; it can appear men only like sex. It is simply not true. Well, men liking sex is true, but women also have red in them. They merely have a different hue of red that needs to be understood.

Several factors could be *fading* the "red" in your spouse. It could be past trauma, hormone levels, stress from work or finances, kids acting out, unmet needs, feeling overwhelmed, sheer exhaustion—or, let's be real, maybe it's just that time of the month. All these things can pile up and dim the vibrant red that once burned bright.

Are some of these issues impacting your spouse currently? Do you talk about them? What is the key to your partner's hue of red? What will deeply satisfy your partner in the bedroom?

Let these questions be a lifetime of curiosity for you. You will never figure out the answer. This is the mystery. It's these fundamental differences that paint the vibrant hues of red in a marriage.

In Chapter 5, we will talk more about sexual intimacy. There is no one way to discover the sexual desires of your spouse. You have to get wildly curious about their emotions, body, and soul. But it is worth the curiosity.

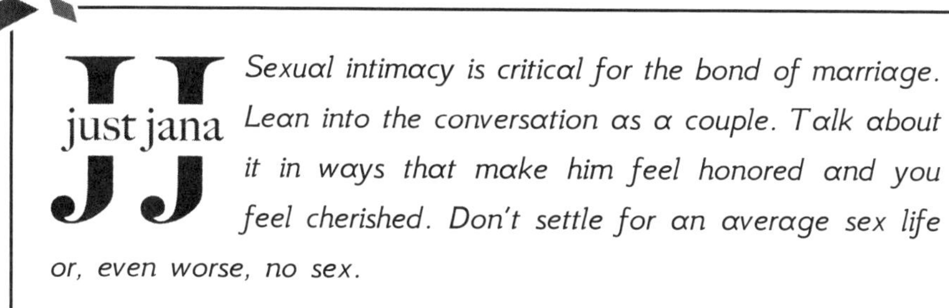

Sexual intimacy is critical for the bond of marriage. Lean into the conversation as a couple. Talk about it in ways that make him feel honored and you feel cherished. Don't settle for an average sex life or, even worse, no sex.

Yellow | Warmth and Communication

Yellow, the color of warmth and communication, symbolizes clarity, optimism, and the flow of ideas and thoughts between partners. Healthy communication is where both partners feel understood and valued.

There is no doubt men and women have different hues of yellow.

Men tend to communicate to solve problems. They listen to fix, to act, to conquer the issue at hand. Women communicate to discover problems. They like to feel it before they fix it. Women use dialogue as a means to explore emotions, understand nuances, and build connections.

Ladies, why does your man communicate differently than you? Is it because he is insensitive? Why does he love to solve problems and fix things? Why does he have a hard time giving you his undivided attention? Instead of trying to fix him, become wildly curious about how your man communicates. He has Yellow inside of him. You have to discover how to get him to communicate.

Men, why does your lady seem to communicate easier than you? At times, it seems all she is doing is talking around problems instead of solving them. Why is she different from you? Let these questions strike a curiosity in your heart. Instead of responding with frustration, respond with wild curiosity.

Ok, confession time: I can't tell you how I still get this wrong, even after 35 years of marriage! Jana starts talking, her face clouded with frustration about her rough day at work. My mind immediately goes into fix-it mode. "Have you tried organizing your tasks differently?" "Have you created a to-do list?" (I create a to-do list for everything, even on my days off). As I look at her, I can see the energy leave her body. It hits me— I'm not giving her the warmth and brightness she needs. Jana wants me to listen, not pull out my whiteboard and begin to brainstorm solutions like I'm running a Fortune 500 company. She isn't looking for solutions; she needs me to listen, not to lecture.

I wish I could say I never do this. But Jana and I are writing this book together, and she would laugh if I made this claim. I do my best.

Here is another question to help you become wildly curious about your spouse: what hue of yellow is your spouse's communication style?

What is their love language? One of the books that has helped us grow in the yellow of marriage is *The Five Love Languages* by Gary Chapman. It is definitely worth reading, as it describes 5 different hues.

The five love languages or hues of yellow are:

1. Words of affirmation
2. Quality time
3. Physical touch
4. Acts of service
5. Receiving gifts

Every Monday night, like clockwork, Jana looks at me and says, "You know what today is . . ." She's reminding me that Tuesday morning is garbage day, and it's my job to take the cans to the curb. On those rare occasions when I get ahead of her and take out the garbage without her prompting, I'm speaking her love language loud and clear. For her, this act communicates love. I don't quite get it—if she wants that kind of reaction from me, she needs to show up naked! We have different love languages! My love language is words of affirmation and physical touch, and Jana's is acts of service.

Is this frustrating? It absolutely is! But this is the beauty of your mosaic. You have to become wildly curious about your spouse . . . what circumstances change the hue of yellow?

Blue | Calm and Emotional Connection

Blue, the color of calm and depth, symbolizes the emotional connection in marriage. It represents trust, loyalty, and the profound connections that bind the mosaic together.

Yes, you guessed it . . . both men and women have blue inside of them . . . they just have different hues of blue.

For men, their primary emotional need is respect. Respect is not merely a preference but a fundamental need that fuels their sense of worth and identity. When a man feels respected, he is empowered, confident, valued, and motivated to invest more deeply in the relationship. This is why men return to success. They need to hear, "Good job." Compliment a man on a job well done, and watch him light up. On the other hand, women desire love, an emotional connection that assures them of their significance and cherished place in the relationship. For them, love and respect is one of the same. Yes, women need respect. If a woman feels taken for granted, this can cause them to feel disrespected or not loved. For them—in most instances—many times it is one and the same. When they feel love—they feel respected.

Ladies, why does your man like to be complimented, praised, and respected? Is this because he is narcissistic, or did God create him like this? Is this normal—a good need for your man? Be wildly curious about the answer to these questions. Not for all men, but your man!

Men, why does your wife need your heart? Why are the words "I love you" so meaningful for your wife? Why can she say "I love you" and have no ulterior motive to go to the bedroom? This is foreign to you. Why? Get curious. Stop being frustrated and direct that energy toward learning about her.

The phrase "Happy wife, happy life" does a disservice to both the wife and the husband. It implies that the wife is high-maintenance or a bit controlling, as if her happiness is just a tool to keep the peace, reducing her feelings to a mere strategy rather than something genuine. It boxes her into the stereotype of the perpetually unhappy woman. At the same time, it sidelines the husband's happiness, making it seem like his well-being is just an afterthought. This mindset undermines the true partnership that marriage is meant to be.

It's time to toss this outdated saying and embrace the reality that both partners' emotional well-being is equally vital. A thriving life together isn't just about keeping one person happy—it's about both of you showing up, caring for each other, and finding joy in the journey together.

In truth, both partners in a marriage bring their own "hues of blues"—those moments of stress, sadness, or dissatisfaction. Ignoring one in favor of the other is a recipe for disaster. A thriving marriage isn't about just one person being happy; it's about both partners feeling seen, heard, and valued.

> **JJ just jana** *Ladies, don't be fooled—men have hues of blue in their emotional spectrum, too. They crave emotional connection, though their hues of blue might look different from yours. I have learned Troy's emotions. Troy and I connect better when we're not sitting face-to-face with me demanding, "Talk to me." Instead, he opens up while we're driving, taking a walk, or engaging in deep philosophical or theological discussions. So be wildly curious how your man communicates. What is the best time?*

Stress and Emotions

It's tough to talk about the hues of blue without talking about stress. Stress and emotions are companions of one another.

Stress and success both impact a man's emotions. This is why men retreat to their "cave" to deal with stress. They want to be by themselves when life is overwhelming. The hues of blue can change for a man depending on his career, successes, how he feels about life, and the economy. The hues don't stay the same.

When a woman's emotions are not being met, she can go into a deep hole, what I call a well. She can go deep. The worst thing a man can do is stand at the rim of the well and yell, "Come out, it's fine!" It only echoes back, pushing her further into the shadows.

When your wife is discouraged and deep in the well, don't say:

- "Don't worry."

- "It's not a big deal."

- "Look at what I have given you."

- "That's not what I said."

- "I'm sorry. Forget the whole thing."

- "We do talk. What are we doing now?"

- "You shouldn't feel hurt."

These words will only push her further down in the well. Go down into the well and say, "Tell me more," "I am listening," and then actually listen.

Ladies, why does your man retreat to his cave when feeling emotionally stressed? Why does he want to be by himself when he is stressed? Men, why does your lady go to the well? What are signs she is in the well? What does she need from you when in the well? All these questions should cause you to be wildly curious about the depth of your spouse.

JJ just jana *Often, the very things that attract us to our spouse are our differences—the unique hues within each of our color wheels. But once we're married, those same differences can start to drive us crazy. Yet, it's these differences that bring beauty to your marriage. Embrace them, blend them, and create something extraordinary. Just like mixing paint, you'll discover a new hue you never expected. It's actually a beautiful masterpiece that you are creating.*

QUICK MARRIAGE TEST: NAPKIN EDITION #1

Grab a coffee and a napkin—yes, a napkin. You're about to do something that could change your marriage in less time than it takes to finish that latte.

On the napkin, write three words: Red, Yellow, Blue.

Now, here's the test. Privately, on a scale of 1 to 10, score your marriage in these three areas:

- Red: Sexual Intimacy – How connected do you feel physically?

- Yellow: Communication – How well are you talking with each other?

- Blue: Emotional Needs – How well are your deepest feelings being met?

Take a moment, jot down your numbers, and keep them to yourself for now. Then, when you're both ready, compare your scores. Are they the same? Probably not. That's okay—it's actually good. This isn't about pointing fingers or winning; it's about opening a conversation.

Discuss why your scores differ. What's behind those numbers? Is there a gap between what you need and what you're getting? What do those differences say about your marriage?

Remember, this isn't a pass/fail test. It's a way to talk about the things that really matter, and maybe, just maybe, it'll lead to a stronger, more colorful marriage.

BLEND, DON'T BEND

When you hear the word 'compromise,' it feels like a concession—a small part of yourself slipping away in the process. It's like settling for a color that doesn't quite match, a hue that's just a bit off from what you truly envisioned.

Most marriage books will tell you to compromise, but let's be real: compromise often leaves one person feeling shortchanged, like they've given up something essential. I'm going to go against the grain here—don't compromise. Instead, try this: blend, don't bend.

When you blend two colors, you're not watering down the originals; you're creating something entirely new. Those original colors don't disappear. They're still there, adding depth, richness, and vibrancy to a fresh, unique hue. Blending isn't about losing yourself; it's about enhancing what you both bring to the table.

Think of your marriage as a color palette. You bring your colors, your spouse brings theirs, and together, you create a masterpiece that's uniquely yours. Each brushstroke adds depth, each shade highlights something different in the other. Blending your colors doesn't erase your individuality; it amplifies it.

In marriage, blending means you're both actively contributing to something bigger. It's about adding to the mix, not subtracting. When you blend, you're not just coasting along—you're crafting a shared life that's richer, deeper, and more beautiful than anything you could create alone.

So don't bend—blend. Together, you'll create a palette more stunning than you ever imagined

HOW TO OVERCOME BEING COLORBLIND

I'm colorblind. You're colorblind. We see the colors we're programmed to see. My wife sees yellow in me when I'm clearly in the red, and I see red in her when she's shining yellow. How do we overcome this colorblindness? There's only one way: become wildly curious about your spouse! Learn everything you can about their red, blue, yellow, and every hue in between.

Alright, let's get practical. How do you become wildly curious about your spouse?

Listen | Give Your Undivided Attention

The goal is to give your spouse your undivided attention—not the kind where you nod while mentally planning tomorrow's to-do list, but the kind where you make eye contact and resist the urge to interrupt with your own stories. It's called active listening.

Listening is an art, and in marriage, it's a superpower. My number one piece of wisdom for men is this: Listen—don't solve problems. Trust me, just shutting your mouth and listening pays big dividends in your marriage.

When your wife starts talking, and you're unsure what to say, stay silent. Instead, lean in and say things like, "Tell me more," "I'm listening," or "I'm here." Even if it feels forced, nod, smile, and throw in an occasional "Tell me more"—it works wonders. But remember, this isn't about just checking a box; sincerity is key. If you're not genuine, she'll see right through it, and it won't have the impact you're hoping for.

Just the other day, I was holed up in a hotel room, pouring my heart into writing this book on marriage, when a minor family issue popped up. Jana, not wanting to disturb me, devised her own plan of action. When I finally returned, she began explaining the problem. My fix-it instincts kicked in immediately, and I started offering my own ideas. As I spoke, I saw the energy drain from her face. She looked deflated, like a balloon losing air. I caught myself mid-sentence, took a deep breath, and instead of barreling forward with my "brilliant" solutions, I said, "Tell me more." She smiled, knowing this came straight from the book, but appreciated that I caught myself.

Simple, right? But oh, so powerful.

Learn | Get a PhD in Your Spouse

Listening is only half the battle. Now you need to really learn.

It's time to get a PhD in your spouse. Getting a PhD means committing to lifelong learning. Think of yourself as an eternal student. Your spouse is the most fascinating subject you could ever study. You'll never graduate, and that's a good thing! There's always something new to learn, some hidden layer to uncover.

How do you get a PhD in your spouse? You need to take a class: Pay Attention 101. Pay attention to their likes and dislikes, their fears, dreams, and everything in between. Notice their rhythms, their quirks, and what makes them tick. Be aware of the subtle changes in their moods, recognize when they need support, and celebrate their victories, big and small.

The second class you need to take is Ask Questions 201. Learn to ask meaningful, open-ended questions that invite your spouse to share their thoughts, dreams, and feelings.

Start with the Couples Chat at the end of each chapter. These questions are designed to help you learn more about each other.

The third class is Learn Their World 301. This is where you dive into their world. This means participating in their interests and passions, even if they're not your cup of tea.

For 35 years, Jana and I have been taking these classes over and over again. In every season of life—from newly married, young kids, teenage kids, and empty nesters—these classes have helped us discover new things about each other. Like visiting the Grand Canyon, it never gets old.

just jana

Troy and I decided to do something we have never done after 35 years of marriage. We rented a 40-foot RV and traveled across Idaho, Montana, Utah, and Arizona, visiting Bryce Canyon, the Grand Canyon, and embarking on all kinds of adventures. We learned so much about each other just by doing something different. Our counselor recommended we do some high-intensity activities. Let's just say we took the counselor literally. We did horseback riding, rappelling in canyons, riding Razrs, and taking a helicopter ride. Unsurprisingly, our counselor hit the nail on the head. Those high-energy activities not only helped us unplug from the stress of life but also recaptured the beauty of our love.

Lionize | Celebrate your Spouse

I don't know about you, but 'lionize' sounds like it should be a romantic word, doesn't it? Try this: go home tonight and say to your spouse, 'Honey, tonight I want to lionize you.' I'm pretty sure they'll respond with, 'What does that even mean?' At that point, you might want to have a dictionary handy—or just be ready to backpedal and suggest dinner instead.

Lionize means to treat someone as a celebrity, to give them an abundance of public attention and approval.[9] It implies celebrating and praising someone highly, treating them with great importance. The word "lionize" comes from the practice of treating someone like a lion, a symbol of power and significance. This usage originated in the early 19th century. In the past, lions were often central attractions in exhibitions, drawing admiration and attention, just as people who are lionized do.

JJ just jana *When the girls were young, I taught them a song: "Let's talk about Daddy, our very special guy, he is so wonderful, so kind, and caring. Let's talk about Daddy everyday." I taught my girls to lionize their dad. Why? Troy is my hero. He is my lion. Lionize your husband. Never speak ill of him; celebrate him.*

Here are some thoughtful ways to lionize your partner and strengthen your bond:

Every spouse wants to feel like the lion or lioness of their home. Here's how you make that happen:

- Speak well of them in front of the kids: Let them hear you say, "Your dad is amazing because . . ." "you have the best mom to ever live."

- Express gratitude: Regularly tell your husband, "Thank you for providing for our family," recognizing his hard work. Tell your wife "I appreciate you caring for our family."

- Encourage him: Be his cheerleader, offering words that uplift and empower.

- Showcase his qualities: Use social media to share his accomplishments and your pride in him.

- Social media & public life: I'm not shy about lionizing Jana publicly. Whether it's on social media or in any public setting, I proudly shout her importance and value to anyone who will listen. She's my queen, and I make sure the world knows it.

- Become an advocate: Support your spouse's personal and professional growth. Encourage them to pursue their passions, offer help when needed, and celebrate their successes.

Let's get real for a moment. Giving Jana my undivided attention doesn't come naturally—I have to be intentional about it every single day. Learning more about her takes effort; I can't just coast through life on autopilot. It's not like I can say, "Hey Siri, teach me about Jana." No, it takes focus, commitment, and a whole lot of love to truly *lionize* her.

For me, this intentionality isn't just a one-time thing; it's a daily practice. The more I intentionally engage with Jana, the more it becomes second nature to listen, learn, and lionize her throughout the week. But it starts with being deliberate.

PRESENT YOUR SPOUSE BACK TO CHRIST

Now, here's a question that often comes up: if we're not here to fix or change our spouse, then how do we help them grow? I thought we were supposed to help our spouse grow and address their weaknesses. Do we just discover who they are and accept them completely without any effort to help them change? The answer isn't about turning a blind eye; it's about loving them through the process. It's about supporting their growth, not forcing it. Real change happens in an environment of love and grace, not control and criticism.

Fascinating question. Here's the thing: your spouse isn't your project. They're not your child who needs to be taught, your client who needs guidance, or someone you're mentoring, coaching, or consulting.

They are the love of your life. Your husband or wife. You share a bond with them that you have with no one else.

After 35 years of marriage, I certainly hope Jana has become a better person. And trust me, being married to her has made me more of a man of character and substance. But here's the key: this growth comes from humility, learning together, and blending our colors into a beautiful mosaic.

When God gave me Jana, she was His daughter first. My greatest hope and prayer is that one day I'll present Jana back to Christ better than He gave her to me. I want my Savior to be pleased with how I treated His daughter. But let's be clear—this isn't about fixing or changing her; it's about discovering her and bringing out her best. Will changes happen? You better believe it. Life changes us. Life shapes us. She was 19 when I married her, and I was 22. We've grown up together, transitioning from youth to adults, hand in hand. Today, we're both richer, better, and more like Christ than we were as those young kids in love—though I still can't believe she said yes!

JJ just jana Pro Tip for Men: How to listen to your lady.

Ok, men, this one's for you. Ever wonder how to truly listen to your lady? Take it from a woman: when you take the time to really listen, she'll feel loved, and guess what? She'll love you right back in ways that'll blow your mind.

Here are seven simple ways to listen to your lady:

1. Ask, Then Listen

    Yes! You heard me. Ask her how she's doing—and then be quiet and actually *listen*. Don't jump in with solutions, fixes, or advice unless she specifically asks for it. Just be present. Silence is golden, fellas. It's her moment, not your monologue.

2. Listen with Your Eyes

    When she's talking, don't just hear her—*see* her. Put the phone down, pause the game, close your laptop, and make eye contact. Show her that she's got your full, undivided attention. Believe me, she'll know if you're truly dialed in or just pretending.

3. Repeat What You Hear

    No, this isn't some kind of psychology hack—it works. When she finishes, repeat back what you heard in your own words. It shows that you're not just hearing but understanding her. "So, you're saying…" goes a long way. She'll feel valued, not dismissed.

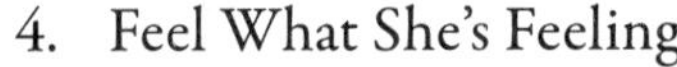

4. Feel What She's Feeling

   Empathy, guys. It's not just for therapy sessions. Tune in to her emotions. If she's excited, get excited with her. If she's frustrated, let her know you feel that too. Emotional connection is the key to unlocking deeper intimacy.

5. Ask the Follow-Up Question

   Don't let the conversation die. When she's done talking, ask a follow-up question. It shows you care about more than just "getting through" the conversation. Dive deeper into what she's saying. She'll love that you're genuinely engaged.

6. Go Into the Well with Her

   This one is crucial. When she's in a tough spot—emotionally or mentally—don't stand at the top of the well and yell down, trying to fix things from above. Get down there with her. Sit in that moment, feel what she's feeling. This will bring her out quicker than you think. (More on this in Chapter 3—don't miss it.)

7. Celebrate the Small Wins

   Don't brush off the little stuff. If she shares a small victory, make a big deal out of it. Celebrate the tiny moments, not just the major milestones. It shows you value everything she says and does, not just the headline-worthy stuff.

COUPLES CHAT

MARRIAGE EDITION

1. On a scale of 1-10 (1 being low, 10 being high), how curious are you about your spouse today? Has your curiosity grown over time, or has it stagnated? What are some practical ways you can reignite that curiosity about your spouse?

2. In what areas do you find yourself trying to 'fix' or change your spouse? How can you shift your approach to become more curious and appreciative of these differences instead?

3. Reflect on the different 'hues' of red, yellow, and blue in your marriage. How do you and your spouse express passion, communication, and emotional connection differently?

4. How can you better support your spouse's need for respect? For love? What specific actions or words make your spouse feel most valued in these areas?

5. What steps can you take to 'listen, learn, and lionize' your spouse more effectively in your daily life? What new habits or practices could you introduce to make your spouse feel celebrated and appreciated?

6. How do you and your spouse handle stress differently? What can you do to support each other more effectively during stressful times, understanding the differences in how each of you processes stress?

7. What is one area in your spouse's life that you would like to learn more about? How can you intentionally cultivate a deeper curiosity about this aspect of who they are?

ENGAGED EDITION

1. On a scale of 1-10 (1 being low, 10 being high), how curious are you about your fiancé/fiancée today? How has your curiosity changed since you began your relationship?

2. Imagine your future marriage as a color wheel, blending different hues of passion (Red), communication (Yellow), and emotional connection (Blue). How does understanding and blending these primary colors strengthen your future marriage?

3. Do you resonate with the idea that compromise is often overrated, and instead, you need to learn how to blend your differences rather than bending? How does this shift in mindset impact the way you approach challenges in your future marriage?

4. How can you practice better listening skills as a couple? What does it mean to you to give your future spouse your undivided attention?

5. What have you learned about your fiancé/fiancée during your engagement that surprised you? How can you keep learning about each other throughout your marriage?

6. How can you celebrate and "lionize" each other as you prepare for marriage? What specific things can you do or say to make your fiancé/fiancée feel valued, appreciated, and like they're your top priority?

7. Do you resonate with the mindset of wanting to present your spouse back to Christ better than when He gave them to you? How does this perspective shape the way you view your role in your future marriage?

3

SET THE TILES

Have Safe and Secure Conversations

"CAN WE TALK TONIGHT?"

Those four little words can send a chill down any husband's spine. Suddenly, your mind is off to the races: *What did I do this time? Did I forget an anniversary? Leave the toilet seat up—again?* It's like waiting for a jury to deliver a verdict, and you're not even sure what the charges are.

Setting tiles requires precision. You have to apply the glue just right so the tiles stay safe and secure. If that tile isn't properly set, it's only a matter of time before it comes loose or falls off, ruining your masterpiece—and probably causing a few stubbed toes along the way.

Every conversation you have with your spouse works the same way. Just like those tiles, your conversations need to be safe and secure if you want to build a masterpiece.

Safe conversations occur when couples feel comfortable sharing their thoughts and feelings without fear of being hurt or judged. These conversations protect your relationship from the damage of harsh words, criticism, or defensiveness. When both partners feel they can speak openly without fear of rejection or ridicule, it's easier to tackle issues head-on and find solutions together.

Secure conversations are when couples not only feel safe in the moment but also build long-term trust, so they feel confident they can talk about anything now and in the future. This security allows each spouse to fully engage in the conversation, knowing their relationship is a safe haven where love and respect rule the day.

Ultimately, Safe and Secure conversations create a marriage masterpiece—one built on trust, understanding, and mutual respect. They empower both partners to navigate the complexities of married life with confidence, knowing their relationship is a place where they can be fully known and fully loved.

Too often, couples get caught in a cycle of fighting, bickering, and repeating, trapped in a never-ending loop of arguments. But Safe and Secure conversations aren't about winning or losing; they're about bonding your relationship with Gorilla Glue - never losing its grip.

Safe and Secure conversations are where you blend the yellow of warmth and communication with the blue of calm and emotions. With every conversation, these colors mix, resulting in either a vibrant green or a fading hue.

Jana and I live in the Pacific Northwest, where the lush green landscapes symbolize growth and renewal. Imagine your conversations with your spouse feeling just like that fresh scent after a rain—invigorating and life-giving, leaving you both feeling safe and secure in your bond.

This is where secondary colors bring depth to your marriage. When you blend yellow (communication) and blue (emotions), you get a rich, beautiful green in your relationship. Green symbolizes the flourishing connection that comes from safe and secure conversations—where both partners feel valued, growth is nurtured, and optimism fuels your future together. It's that deep sense of peace and progress that only comes when communication and emotions are in sync.

Men and women have different shades of green when it comes to Safe and Secure conversations. Men often set the sprinkler system on auto-pilot, trusting the grass will stay green on its own. Meanwhile, women might prefer to grab an old-fashioned sprinkler, making sure every blade gets the attention it deserves—while discussing the finer points of lawn care, of course. This chapter will help you have Safe and Secure conversations, whether you're a man who likes a sprinkler system or a woman who wants to stand out there and talk it through.

I promise you, if you read this chapter carefully, your conversations can transform from never-ending dialogues to meaningful, Safe and Secure conversations.

FIVE WAYS TO SET THE TILES

When setting the tiles of your relationship, it's not about hammering nails; it's about applying the right amount of glue and making sure they are safe and secure. Nails might seem like they get the job done, but over time, they may cause cracks and damage, leaving your spouse feeling unsafe and insecure. Glue, however, bonds seamlessly, creating a strong and flexible connection that can withstand the pressures of life.

Too many of us love the thrill of being DIY enthusiasts. We dive into our first mosaic project with excitement, armed with a brand-new glue gun and a bag of colorful tiles, ready to create a masterpiece.

But here's what happens next: we apply the glue—way too much of it. We squeeze a generous glob onto each tile, resulting in a sticky mess that's more chaotic than creative. So, we try to correct our mistakes by using less glue. This time, we barely put any on the tiles, and they refuse to stick, falling off with the slightest touch. Frustration sets in as our vision of a masterpiece crumbles before our eyes.

Now, let's talk about how this plays out in your marriage. You might think, "We talked last night," but it didn't stick. Why not? Because, just like in your mosaic, the adhesive wasn't applied correctly. I want to help sincere DIY spouses like you have Safe and Secure conversations—ones that truly bond and hold.

So, let's start setting the tiles of your mosaic—one Safe and Secure conversation at a time. And remember, when she says, "Can we talk tonight?" it's not a setup for a showdown; it's a chance to add another tile to your beautiful masterpiece.

Talk about It Before You Have to Talk about It

It was a perfect day in Pinehurst, Idaho. The sky was clear, and the sun cast a warm glow over the quaint country church where Jana and I were about to exchange our vows. Our journey to this moment had been marked by a special tradition—150 days before our wedding, we started reading the book of Psalms backward, one chapter each day, counting down to our big day. It was a meaningful and spiritual way to prepare for our union.

As the ceremony began, I stood before our friends and family and opened with the reading of Psalm 1. It was a beautiful moment, setting the tone for our celebration. Jana's voice filled the church as she sang the words, "Love comes through every time," her voice carrying the emotions of our love story.

We exchanged our vows and pledges, each word carrying the weight of our covenant love. When I kissed the bride, it was a kiss that sealed our promises to each other. With hearts full of joy, we walked out of that church, hand in hand, ready to start our new life together.

As we got into our car, the excitement and nerves bubbled over. I turned to Jana and, with a grin, said, "Okay, you can touch me now." Don't judge me—I was 22 years old, and my mind was filled with the anticipation of what was to come. My worst fear as a young teenager had been that the rapture would happen and I'd go to heaven a virgin. But now, I was married to the love of my life, and all I could think about was . . . I will stop there.

Yes, he is telling the story right. We got married in Pinehurst, Idaho, and our honeymoon was an hour away in Spokane, Washington. Let's just say this was one exciting drive.

Why was I able to playfully say this? Because sex was not a taboo conversation for us.

From the very beginning of our relationship, Jana and I made it a point to talk openly about sexual intimacy. It's so easy for couples to make assumptions and avoid these conversations.

Before we were married, Jana and I read *The Act of Marriage* by Tim and Beverly LaHaye. It was a practical guide that sparked open conversations about sexual intimacy. By discussing these topics early on, they became way easier when the issue needed to be really talked about. Trust me on this: if you can talk about it before you have to talk about it, then when you talk about it, it'll be way smoother to talk about it (that was a mouthful . . . but you get the idea).

Don't sell yourself short by only talking about problems when you have to; talk about them when they're not happening.

When you proactively engage in a conversation, both partners feel safe and secure—no finger-pointing, no blaming, just honest, open dialogue before issues take root.

Once it's a problem, the discussion gets a whole lot tougher. It's like trying to save your lawn after it's already gone crispy—patches of lifeless brown grass, brittle underfoot, with weeds taking over where the green should be.

Why not talk now and keep things vibrant and thriving? Trust me, it's easier to water your relationship before it looks like a drought hit it.

In appendix E, we have provided a list of the top "Five Intentional Conversations for Couples." By no means is this list exhaustive; it just illustrates some of the top conversations.

JJ just jana *Reading The Act of Marriage was a game-changer for Troy and me. We each took our time with it, reading separately but joining together for some real talk afterward. Troy dove in first, underlining the parts he thought were key—and trust me, that opened up some pretty deep conversations. It gave us a safe space to talk openly about sexual intimacy without all the awkwardness or emotions getting in the way. Now, if you're engaged, take my advice: save this book for 30 days before the wedding. Seriously, you might need to put it down and take a cold shower!*

Go with Who Cares the Most

You can't be married for five minutes without realizing disagreements, conflicts, and downright tensions are part of us becoming a masterpiece. Anytime a couple says, "We never fight," I kind of gag a bit. Either they're not being authentic, or someone is not being heard. Seriously, if you've never had a fight, you're either living in a fairy tale or someone is hiding the remote control of reality.

What do you do when you simply disagree? Drum roll, please . . . Go with who cares the most!

That's it! Problem solved, right?

I wish it were that simple.

In most cases, it should be obvious who cares the most. Decisions like what to have for dinner, which movie to watch, or whether to buy that piece of furniture now or later should be straightforward. But sometimes, they aren't, simply because couples haven't learned to keep focus on what really makes a great mosaic.

They fight over what's for dinner with the same energy they should be using to address why they're not feeling connected. They argue over trivial things and ignore the core issues in their marriage.

Some of us have a broken "care" button—stuck in the "meh" position, obsessing over things that, quite frankly, don't matter a bit. It's like rearranging deck chairs on the Titanic—useless and ridiculous. Let's fix that button and refocus on what truly counts. To be blunt, stop caring about the stupid stuff and start caring about what really matters.

Okay, here's the brutal truth: most of the stuff we argue, bicker, and fight about just doesn't matter. It's small stuff. If you don't think this is true, you might be the one sweating the small stuff in your marriage, and someone needs to tell you.

Small stuff can be things like leaving the toilet seat up, forgetting to take out the trash, misplacing the remote, or minor disagreements about daily routines. These are the trivial issues that, in the grand scheme of things, don't hold much weight but can easily become sources of unnecessary conflict. Instead of letting these small things disrupt your relationship, focus on what truly matters—love, respect, and understanding.

A Third Child

When Jana and I first discussed having a third child, we had been married for four years. I assumed that we would try for a boy. After all, isn't that the natural next step in the grand design of family planning? Jana, however, didn't share my enthusiasm for expanding our family.

We approached this impasse with safe and secure conversations, but the decision wasn't easy. Our discussions were numerous and, yes, occasionally heated. The emotions were raw and real. But never did either of us feel unsafe having this dialogue or uncertain about our future.

Finally, we decided to put the decision on the back burner. Every first of the year, we would revisit the conversation. This wasn't avoiding the conversation; it was a method to allow time and God's wisdom to blend our hearts. We trusted that in the waiting, clarity would come.

By year ten, it became evident that Jana cared more deeply about not having a third child than I did about having one. I deferred to her, not out of resignation, but out of deep love and understanding. Our hues blended. This wasn't a compromise; it was a melding of our desires and dreams.

Also after 10 years, I got tired of wearing condoms.

In the end, our decision not to have a third child was a testament to how God can blend two hues in perfect harmony, even when the journey is long and uncertain.

Going with who cares the most is an act of deferring to one another. It's an act of making your spouse feel safe and secure. It's not about losing; it's about loving. It says to your spouse, "I value your heart and respect you."

The conversation about having a third child was a sensitive one. It became a beautiful test of our mosaic. It would have been easy to say hurtful things to Troy like, 'You're not the one who has to birth the child,' or for him to tell me, 'I was being selfish.' But we didn't. We honored each other and trusted God along the way. Fast forward 35 years, and both of our girls have married amazing sons-in-law, who are like sons to us. Troy is loving every moment and cherishes them as his own.

Set the Temperature

Safe and Secure conversations require you to be a thermostat, not a thermometer, in your marriage. A thermometer just tells you the temperature, but a thermostat? It sets it. You have the power to set the temperature—don't just react to it. Too hot? That's when emotions are high, like a volcano about to blow. Too cold? That's the silent treatment, an emotional ice age where you're distant and disconnected.

Now, don't even think about setting the tile in your marriage unless the temperature is right. If the temperature isn't right, no one's going to feel safe or secure. Timing, tone, and text—they're the thermostat settings you need to consider before any conversation. Get those right, and you'll set the perfect temperature for a safe and secure relationship.

Wait for the Right Time

When you're doing actual tile work, you want the temperature to be within a comfortable range, usually between 50°F and 90°F. Too cold, and the adhesive might not set properly. Too hot, and it might dry too quickly before you can get the tiles in place. In other words, don't talk when your emotions are too hot, too cold . . . or not too hot, not too cold (indifferent). Avoid bringing up sensitive issues during stressful times.

So, if you're feeling like a volcano about to explode or like you're in the middle of an emotional ice age, it might be best to wait for a more temperate moment to set the tiles of your marriage.

I have heard couples say or even push back, "I should be able to say what I want, when I want, and how I want." Well . . . how is that working for you? No one is ready to have Safe and Secure conversations 24 hours a day.

Choose a moment when both of you are calm and not distracted. Examples of bad timing:

1. Late at night: When you're both exhausted and less likely to think clearly or respond calmly.

2. During a family gathering: Don't fight in front of your in-laws or kids.

3. When you're with others: Don't embarrass them—or yourselves.

4. Right after work: When one or both of you might be stressed and mentally drained from the day.

5. During an argument: Emotions are already high, and adding another topic can escalate the conflict.

6. While caring for children: Multitasking with kids around divides attention and increases the likelihood of miscommunication.

7. During meals: This is a time to connect and enjoy each other's company, not hash out conflicts.

8. When either of you is hungry: Nothing is worse than a "hangry" spouse.

JJ just jana

When Troy returns home after a long day, I never greet him with, "can we talk?"—because that's basically code for "brace yourself." Instead, I give him time to unwind. If we need to talk, I wait until we're on a walk or, even better, after he's had a good meal. Timing is everything—because a well-fed man is much more open to conversation and way less likely to flee the scene!

Set the Right Tone

Your tone sets the atmosphere. Tone is the attitude or feeling that your spouse feels through your choice of words, style, and overall approach.

Speak calmly and respectfully, avoiding sarcasm or belittlement. Reflect the principles of love and respect found in 1 Corinthians 13:4-7.

1. Love is patient: Give your spouse time to express their thoughts without interruption.
2. Love is kind: Choose words that are gentle and uplifting.
3. Love is not Proud: Avoid sounding superior or condescending.
4. Love honors: Respect your spouse's feelings and perspectives—even if you disagree.
5. Love is not easily angered: Never be abusive or destructive.
6. Love keeps no records of wrongs: Tear up your naughty list. It will never produce a great marriage.
7. Love trusts and hopes: Stand up for and protect your spouse, both emotionally and physically.

Choose the Right Text (Words)

Your words matter. They set the culture of your marriage and home. Choose them wisely and avoid accusatory language. Ephesians 4:29 advises, "Do not let any unwholesome talk come out of your mouths, but only what is helpful for building others up according to their needs."

Here is a list of actual words Jana and I never say in our marriage because they can crack the mosaic and weaken the glue that holds it together:

1. "I told you so": It's not about being right. It's about being together.

2. "You always/never do this": Using absolute terms like "always" and "never" can make your spouse feel unfairly judged and defensive.

3. "Why can't you be more like (someone else)?": Comparing your spouse to someone else can make them feel inadequate and unappreciated.

4. "It's your fault": Blaming your spouse can lead to defensiveness and resentment.

5. "You're overreacting": Dismissing your spouse's feelings can make them feel invalidated and misunderstood.

6. "You're too sensitive": Dismissing your spouse's emotions can make them feel invalidated and shut down communication.

7. "It's not a big deal": Minimizing your spouse's concerns can make them feel unheard and unimportant.

By avoiding these phrases, you ensure that the glue holding your marriage mosaic together remains strong and intact, allowing your relationship to shine brightly and beautifully.

just jana

The reason some of you don't wait for the right time, set the right tone, or carefully choose your words is simple—you've got an inner bully just itching to come out, or maybe your Wicked Witch of Oz is screaming to be right.

You care more about being right than a healthy relationship. But here's the hard truth: don't blame your spouse for that. It's time to look in the mirror, muster up some courage, and take responsibility for how you handle these conversations. Own it, because that's the only way you'll ever really fix it.

Say It Out Loud

Jana and I have a phrase that helps us with Safe and Secure conversations: "Say it out loud." When we feel gratitude or even some frustrations, we remind each other to "say it out loud." But: Do this at the right time, set the right tone, and carefully choose your words.

Too often, we leave compliments unspoken or words of appreciation unsaid. This simple practice has made a world of difference. By verbalizing our feelings, we ensure that our appreciation is heard and our concerns are addressed before they fester. It's amazing how much closer you feel when you make it a habit to express your thoughts openly and honestly. Very good!

So, don't hold back—say it out loud and watch your connection deepen.

Here are some phrases Jana and I use all the time:

1. "I love you": Never underestimate the power of these three words.

2. "Thank you": Expressing gratitude can transform your relationship.

3. "I appreciate you": Going beyond thank you, this phrase highlights specific qualities and actions that you value in your spouse.

4. "I'm sorry": Apologizing sincerely for mistakes or misunderstandings is crucial. It's the tool that helps repair cracks and ensures your mosaic remains intact.

5. "I believe in you": Encouraging your spouse's dreams and aspirations adds depth to your mosaic.

6. "I need you": Expressing your dependence on your spouse reinforces your bond.

7. "I respect you": Highlighting your respect for your spouse's opinions, choices, and individuality adds a layer of honor to your relationship.

JJ *just jana* — *Ladies, stop nagging your husbands. Proverbs was right: 'Better to live on a corner of the roof than share a house with a quarrelsome wife' (Proverbs 21:9). No wonder your husband wants to go and hide behind the TV. I'm not saying you should avoid bringing things up to your husband. But trust me, timing, tone, and the words you choose make all the difference. Seriously, try what I call the "sandwich model." It's simple—sandwich your comment between two words of encouragement. Here's how it works: "I really appreciate how hard you work. By the way, have you noticed the yard needs mowing? Oh, and I love how you always take care of things around here." And a pro tip—only give him one "to-do" at a time. If you hit him with two, you'll lose him faster than you can say, "Honey-do list."*

Laugh Together

One of the greatest things about my wife is her laugh. But be warned—when Jana laughs, it's a full-on, from-the-gut, belly laugh. I tend to take life and conversations way too seriously, but Jana has this incredible ability to laugh at the days to come, just like Proverbs 31:25 says. And let me tell you, humor in marriage is a game-changer.

Humor isn't just about cracking jokes or watching a funny movie together. It's about finding the absurdities in life, especially when things go sideways. The ability to laugh—really laugh, until your stomach hurts—is like hitting a reset button on your marriage. It's a reminder that our mosaic is made up of broken pieces, and it's those very pieces that come together to create a masterpiece. Proverbs 17:22 says, "A joyful heart is good medicine," and I've seen firsthand that laughter is the medicine that can heal even the deepest wounds in marriage.

But let's get one thing straight—this isn't about laughing at your spouse; it's about laughing with them. Big difference. Laughing at your spouse is like rubbing salt in an open wound; it stings, it burns, and it leaves a scar. But laughing with your spouse? That's like a soothing balm, easing the aches and pains of daily life. It says, "Hey, we're in this together, and no matter what, we can still find joy."

Jana and I learned this principle early in our marriage. One morning, our daughter Kaylee was in her high chair, making a mess of her breakfast. Meanwhile, Jana and I were locked in a trivial argument. I can't even remember what it was about, but you know how it goes—little things become big things in the heat of the moment.

Suddenly, Jana yells, "You never listen to me!" And she's holding a knife—don't worry, it was just a butter knife. Before I could say anything, she slams the knife down on a plate, and the plate shatters into pieces.

We just stared at each other, shocked, surrounded by broken pieces and Kaylee's giggles from her high chair. Then, out of nowhere, Jana starts to laugh—like *really laugh*. Her laughter was contagious, and before long, I was laughing too. We laughed and laughed, right there in the middle of the mess.

In that moment, we realized something crucial: laughter is good. It creates a safe and secure atmosphere. It breaks the tension, heals wounds, and puts everything in perspective. A broken plate isn't the end of the world. It's just a plate.

So, we cleaned up the pieces, kissed, and vowed to pick our battles more wisely. We discovered that sometimes, the best way to glue your relationship back together is with a good dose of laughter and the realization that not every argument is worth the broken plates.

JJ just jana

One very quirky thing about Troy is his uncanny ability to eat the same meal at the same restaurant on the same night of the week—forever. Every Friday night on our date night, like clockwork, we have to stop at Exit 7 for Starbucks coffee. He calls this our special tradition. I call it culinary Groundhog Day. I know I should smile about this and find some humor. . . but really, Troy? I forgot to bring this up to our counselor—probably because I was too busy plotting how to sneak into a new restaurant. What do you think—should I just accept our 'special tradition,' or is it time for a covert operation to spice things up?

Add an Outside Voice

One of the most helpful ways to have Safe and Secure conversations is by bringing in "outside voices" when we need them and often even when we don't. Outside voices can help add beauty to your mosaic by adding new insights into your mosaic.

The truth is most people lack the humility and hunger to engage anyone in their marriage. Humility says, "We don't know it all." Hunger says, "I have enough ambition to actually find an outside voice." Most marriages need a dose of humility and some gasoline in the engine.

When we're stuck, we don't hesitate to bring in an outside voice. Proverbs 11:14 reminds us, "For lack of guidance a nation falls, but victory is won through many advisers"

Here are some ways to bring in outside voices:

- Find marriage mentors: Find couples who have been married for decades and still like each other. They may not be cool or found on Instagram, but they can provide you with down-to-earth insights. Regularly seek their advice and insights. When you meet with these couples, respect their time. If you are out to dinner, pay for the meal. Come with 5-7 questions you want to ask them. Also, don't do much talking. Ask the questions and listen.

- Read and discuss marriage books: You may read them together or even separately and come back and discuss them. We've already mentioned Gary Chapman's *The Five Love Languages*—it is excellent. Recently, we read *Sheet Music: Uncovering the Secrets of Sexual Intimacy* by Kevin Leman. It was a book that helped stretch our minds and hearts around sexual intimacy. And of course, *The Mosaic Marriage* by Troy and Jana Jones is amazing (okay, I might be a bit biased).

- Marriage counseling: So often people feel shame in counseling. We all need an outside perspective. Jana and I recently went to Emerge Ministries in Akron, Ohio. We spent three days discussing our marriage and lives together. It was life-changing!

- Develop trusted friends: One of the key things Jana and I focus on is surrounding ourselves with friends who believe in and celebrate the value of marriage. Study after study proves you are the average of the five people you spend the most time with. In other words, if the top five people you hang out with are negative about marriage . . . you will become that.

When we went through our seven-year wake-up call, I decided to focus on couples married for 30+ years and watch them and learn from them. They taught me that being married is not all the fancy stuff but loving each other day after day, year after year, and decade after decade.

For all the introverts out there, the thought of talking to someone about your marriage can feel like a nightmare. Troy loves this stuff—he could talk to a brick wall and call it therapy. Me? Not so much. But here's my advice—stretch yourself and give it a try. You might be surprised. And if not, at least you can say you gave it a shot! But honestly, you can still be mentored by people you've never even met. Follow them on Instagram, listen to their podcasts, or attend a marriage conference. You don't have to sit down face-to-face to get the wisdom—you can learn while in your pajamas!

Rick and Susan Ross

One of the greatest outside voices in our lives are Rick and Susan Ross. They became pastors of New Life Church the year Jana and I got married. Neither of us came from a minister's family, although Jana's mom and stepfather were loyal church members and understood the life of a church.

Rick and Susan Ross stepped into our lives and became perhaps one of the greatest outside voices we have to this day. They taught us the personal and professional sides of marriage and ministry. How to dress as ministers, how to conduct yourself, how to be married, and so much more.

Rick personally taught me how to lead a church and not get lost in the weeds of the congregation. He also taught me finances. He taught and, perhaps more importantly, showed me how to spend money, save for the future, and pay attention to financial management. I look at the strength of my finances today, and it is because of this outside voice . . . someone who cared.

Okay, let's start setting some tiles in your mosaic. What are those Safe and Secure conversations you need to have? Go have them!

ProTip for both partners:

just jana *Seven "Nevers" When Talking to Your Spouse*

1. Never get defensive:

   Defensiveness can shut down a conversation. Instead, stay open and receptive to feedback, even if it's hard to hear.

2. Never raise your voice:

   Yelling only escalates conflict. Proverbs 15:1 reminds us that "a gentle answer turns away wrath."

3. Never blame:

   Focus on expressing your feelings rather than blaming your partner. Use "I" statements instead of "You" accusations.

4. Never bring up the past:

   Stick to the issue at hand. Bringing up past mistakes can derail the conversation and prevent resolution.

5. Never make assumptions:

   Don't assume you know what your spouse is thinking or feeling. Ask questions and seek to understand.

6. Never use sarcasm:

    Sarcasm can be hurtful and is often misunderstood. Aim for clear, respectful communication instead.

7. Never use absolute language:

    Words like "always" and "never" are rarely true and often inflammatory. Avoid them to prevent escalation. Of course, it's okay to use the word 'never' when you're writing a section called 'Seven Nevers When Talking To Your Spouse.'

COUPLES CHAT

MARRIAGE EDITION

1. On a scale of 1-10 (1 being low, 10 being high), how safe do you feel with your spouse right now? Why? How secure do you feel in your relationship? Why? Take a moment to rate it and discuss your answers together.

2. What are some topics you think should be discussed proactively before they become problems? How can you make time for these conversations in your relationship?

3. When you and your spouse disagree, how do you decide who "cares the most" about the issue? How can you ensure that both of your perspectives are respected in the process?

4. How do you typically approach timing, tone, and text (words) during difficult conversations? What changes could you make to ensure that these conversations remain safe and secure?

5. Do you agree that laughter is good medicine for a marriage? How can you and your spouse cultivate the ability to laugh together more often? What are some new ways you can infuse humor into your relationship?

6. What outside voices (mentors, books, counselors, trusted friends) have been helpful in your marriage? How can you incorporate more of these voices to strengthen your relationship?

7. How can you encourage each other to "say it out loud"—expressing gratitude, appreciation, or concerns—while ensuring that the timing, tone, and words are chosen wisely?

ENGAGED EDITION

1. On a scale of 1-10 (1 being low, 10 being high), how safe do you feel sharing your thoughts and feelings with your future spouse? How secure do you feel in your relationship, knowing you can talk about anything?

2. What are some topics you think should be discussed proactively before they become problems? How can you make time for these conversations and ensure that both of you feel comfortable discussing even sensitive issues early on?

3. When you and your future spouse disagree, how do you decide who "cares the most" about the issue? How can you both ensure that your perspectives are valued without letting trivial matters become sources of conflict?

4. Reflect on how you typically handle the timing, tone, and choice of words during difficult conversations. What adjustments can you make to ensure your discussions remain respectful and productive, especially when dealing with sensitive topics?

5. Do you agree that laughter can be a healing force in your relationship? How can you and your future spouse cultivate the ability to laugh together more often?

6. What outside voices (mentors, books, counselors, trusted friends) have been influential in your relationship? How can you seek out more of these voices?

7. How comfortable are you with expressing gratitude, appreciation, or concerns in your relationship? How can you encourage each other to "say it out loud" more often?

4

FILL IN THE GAPS

Do the Finish Work

YOU'VE FINALLY COMPLETED THAT JAW-DROPPING kitchen remodel. You've invested a small fortune, and you're beaming with pride. Then someone, with a mix of admiration and hesitation, whispers, "Your kitchen looks amazing, but . . ." They pause. Your heart skips a beat. You quickly ask, "What is it?" They hesitantly reply, "Well . . . whoever did your grout work didn't know what they were doing."

You lean in for a closer look, and there it is—the grout between the tiles—cracked, uneven, and, in some spots, completely missing. Tiny gaps expose the wall beneath, an eyesore in an otherwise perfect scene.

Ouch. That's a gut punch.

But it's just grout, right? No big deal?

This is exactly how many marriages look—beautifully clean on the surface, with the tiles perfectly set, but the grout? It's a hot mess. The finish work was done so quickly and sloppily, you'd think it was a race against the clock.

Not all contractors are good with finish work. Why? Because it's detailed and takes time—and let's face it, nobody likes dealing with those tiny gaps.

But here's the kicker: the finish work is what really makes a mosaic shine. So, if your marriage is starting to resemble a DIY project gone wrong, it might be time to break out the grout and get to work!

MIND THE GAP

Ever heard the phrase "mind the gap"? Straight from the London Underground, it's a warning for commuters to watch their step—because a small gap between the train and the platform can turn your daily routine into an unexpected disaster.

In marriage, it's the same—those tiny gaps that creep in over the years can trip you up faster than you think. So unless you're auditioning for a marriage blooper reel, it's time to fill in those gaps and avoid a fall that's more than just embarrassing.

Filling the gaps is more than just maintenance; it's protection. Finish work guards the edges of your marriage, keeping the dirt and grime from creeping in.

Left unattended, small gaps can turn into gaping chasms. Over time, they weaken the foundation of your relationship.

Finish work isn't glamorous. It's meticulous, detailed work. It's the behind-the-scenes effort that often goes unnoticed, but makes all the difference. So, you ask, "What's 'Finish work'?" The goodnight kisses, the morning coffees, the "just because" text messages are a few examples. These small, consistent actions help keep your marriage strong.

So, grab your grout gun, and let's fill those gaps. Trust me, there's no fun in tripping over what should have been a solid, beautiful mosaic.

> **JJ** **just jana** *One of Troy's superpowers is his knack for taking complicated things and breaking them down into simple, clear steps that anyone can follow. He's got a Google Doc for everything—our values, vision, and goals are all laid out in black and white. It's how we stay on the same page in every core area of our lives. So, buckle up and enjoy, because in this chapter, you're going to see that superpower in action. And trust me, after 35 years of marriage, I can promise you'll benefit from it just like I have.*

FAITH: THE SPIRITUAL GAP

Couples should have devotions together, right? Well, in the spirit of total transparency . . . this doesn't work for us. *[Some of you might be gasping right now.]*

We figured this out on our honeymoon, of all places. As a proud new husband, I eagerly opened the Bible and started reading aloud, complete with my "preacher" observations. Jana quickly cut me off, clearly annoyed. "Just read it, don't talk about it," she said. My first reaction? Defensiveness. But in that moment, I discovered something crucial—Jana and I connect with God in totally different ways.

Jana's approach to the Bible is devotional. She savors each word, soaking it in without distractions—even from her brilliant husband. I, on the other hand, read the Bible like it's a gripping story, engaging with it as intensely as I would with my favorite Netflix show. But this interactive style? Yeah, it doesn't suit Jana.

Prayer is another area where we differ. When Jana prays, it's like a thunderstorm—powerful, intense, sending every demon running for cover. I love her passion for prayer. My approach? It's more like a gentle sprinkling rain. It can turn into a thunderstorm, but it takes a little time.

When it comes to our walk with God, Jana and I definitely have different colors and hues. We've learned to deeply appreciate this about each other. We don't try to change or fix one another; we just listen and learn with wild curiosity.

So, what works for us? How do we blend these colors? Instead of reading the Bible together, we read the same Bible reading plan on The Bible app individually. We share our thoughts in the app and then discuss what we've read throughout the day. This approach keeps us connected without stepping on each other's toes.

As for prayer, we pray as a family when the adult kids leave the house or when there's an obvious need. Jana and I will also listen to guided prayers together, and then I'll pray afterward. Occasionally, I'll record a personal prayer and text it to her, which she loves.

Spiritual hunger will protect the edges, fill in the gaps, and keep the dirt from creeping in.

just jana JJ

Ladies, over the years I have learned when our men try to lead us spiritually, we need to let them do it on their terms, within their comfort zone. This is not the time to unleash your charismatic wild side—save that for the bedroom. Show your man patience and love, fruits of the Spirit. Why is it that we can be outwardly charismatic but inwardly judgmental toward our husbands? Just something to ponder.

Numerous well-known sociologists, demographers, psychologists, and researchers have found that when someone is active in their faith, it significantly lowers their chances of divorce. This is an amazing tribute to followers of Jesus.[10]

The greatest way to ensure your marriage becomes a masterpiece is to have an authentic faith—a faith that isn't tucked away within the walls of a building or hidden behind the curtain of religion. Your marriage should be the first place where this genuine faith shines bright. Let your family see what it truly means to follow Jesus wholeheartedly. Let your spouse and kids witness the gospel in action through your own life.

And here's something else to consider: among Christians who had attended church in the last seven days, the divorce rate was 27 percent lower.[11] The quickest way to extinguish a fire is to separate the logs. The same is true for your spiritual fire. The enemy wants to isolate you, to pull you away from the very community that strengthens you. You need to find a home church and get connected. Don't let your faith flicker out—let it burn bright in the heart of your marriage.

JJ just jana

We love the local church. Our kids and grandkids love the church. So please, don't let anyone tell our kids and grandkids that the church is full of hypocrites or that it's riddled with problems. We tell them, "Yes, we're all sinners; we're all a hot mess." But here's the beauty—God takes our broken pieces and turns our lives into masterpieces. And God uses His church, His people—all the broken people who attend, including us—to become the hope of the world. That's the church we love.

By the way, the greatest gift you can give your kids is helping them engage in a home church. Their lives will be forever shaped by it.

FAMILY: THE HOME GAP

We live in a world that glorifies busyness. From the moment we wake up, it's a race against time—emails, texts, meetings, deadlines, errands, and the constant buzz of notifications. But amidst the chaos, there's one place that should be our sanctuary, our safe haven: home.

There is no place like home. And no, I'm not talking about Dorothy clicking her shoes together and saying a pretty little statement. Sure, her ruby slippers and that magical phrase got her back to Kansas, but home is much more than a ticket out of Oz.

Home is a fortress of meaning and beauty. It's the place that protects the edges of your lives, fills in the gaps, and prevents dirt from getting in. Home is where we learn not to let the world's moisture turn us into mold.

This section of the book is personal for me. I came from a broken family. I had no sense of family. So, when I got married, I was clueless.

Here are ways to fill in the family gap:

Put Your Marriage First

A strong family starts with a rock-solid marriage. Without it, your family will feel the cracks. The best thing a father can do for his kids? Love their mom like crazy.

So, how do you keep that marriage strong? Here are some ways to fill in the gaps and add the necessary grout to your marriage masterpiece.

- Date Night: For 35 years, we've made date night a non-negotiable. It's our sacred time. This is the day we do errands together, sip coffee, catch up on life, go out for dinner, and then just enjoy each other's company. During this time, Jana gets my full, undivided attention. No distractions, no half-hearted conversations—just us.

- Getaways: Jana and I make it a point to have our own getaways, just the two of us. We even have a second home in Chelan, Washington, specifically for this purpose. It's our retreat, our place to reconnect and recharge without the noise of everyday life.

- Evening Walks: As we've gotten older, our evening walks have become one of our favorite ways to connect. These walks are more than just exercise; they're intentional moments where we give each other our full attention, deepening our connection with every step.

> **JJ** **just jana** *One of the most intentional things Troy and I have done for 35 years is prioritize date night. While I often felt guilty leaving the kids, Troy was intentional about finding sitters. But he didn't just find babysitters; he found people who became part of our extended family. Members of our church stepped in, becoming uncles, aunts, grandmas, and grandpas. They didn't just watch our kids—they loved them.*

Lionize Your Spouse When Kids Arrive

It's easy to slip into a kid-centric marriage, where you unintentionally sideline the love of your life. Now, don't get me wrong—your kids (or grandkids) are the heartbeat of your home. But the best way to love them? Take care of your marriage first!

Think about it: one day, those kids will fly the coop, and you'll find yourselves as empty nesters. Do you want a marriage that merely (hopefully) survives the transition or one that thrives well into your golden years?

It's about harmony, not balance. Balance is overrated—it implies everything is equal all the time. Harmony, on the other hand, means everything gets the attention it needs, exactly when it needs it. Sure, there will be moments when the kids need to take center stage, and that's okay. But even in those moments, let your kids know that their mom or dad is still the star of the show. If your spouse walks into the room, they should feel like the world just stopped to take notice. Okay, maybe we're not literally asking the kids to stand and salute, but you get the point.

Ask your spouse, "Do you feel like I value you more than anything in the world, even more than our kids?" Then, listen. Learn. And lionize them. Even when you're knee-deep in diapers or playing Uber driver for the next church event or soccer game, make sure your spouse still feels like a lion / lioness.

Family Nights

Family nights are intentional evenings or specific blocks of time that you and your spouse agree on—those moments when you both say, "We will be home together tonight." Depending on your job, this can be challenging. Some of you travel for a living; others, like me, have a job where evenings are required. We are in full-time ministry, where many evenings are devoted to church or meeting people's needs. For you, it might mean thinking in terms of blocks of time rather than a rigid weekly schedule. Whatever it takes, make this work for you.

Early in our marriage, I'll confess, we started with just three nights a week dedicated to family time. We thought we were doing pretty well! But as the years passed, we realized the deep impact of these moments together and gradually increased to 4-5 nights weekly. It's not about meeting a specific quota; it's about consistently choosing to prioritize your family.

So, what does this commitment look like in practice? It might mean declining that extra work event, skipping a gym session, or passing on a night out with friends. These are all good things, no doubt, but they pale in comparison to the lasting value of being present at home, creating memories, and nurturing the relationships that matter most.

Table Moments

Table moments are those priceless times when everyone gathers around the table—whether for a meal, a board game, or just to talk. These moments might seem simple, but they're the glue that holds families together, creating a rhythm of connection, communication, and belonging.

One of our favorite family traditions every summer is spending five days together in Chelan—yes, the whole Jones tribe. Picture it: six adults, five grandkids, and a whole lot of fun! It's a blast. We've got a family rule: I cover the meals, and the sons-in-law handle the cooking. And let me tell you, they can cook! It's a full-on feast, like dining as kings and queens every day.

One of the things we do that's become a tradition over the years is putting everyone's name in a jar. After each meal, we pick two names—usually one of the grandkids gets to do the honors—and then we all take turns sharing why we appreciate those two people. It's such a special time, filled with love and gratitude around the table. After we're done, I typically pray for the names that were picked.

It's more than just a meal. It's a moment.

Think of table moments as intentional gatherings that happen around the table. It could be breakfast before the day kicks off, dinner after a long day, or a game night where the table transforms into a battlefield of fun. But let's be clear—these moments aren't just about sharing food; they're about sharing life. They're a chance to hit pause, connect, and really listen to each other.

Table moments create a sacred space where meaningful conversations happen, and everyone gets their turn to be heard. These gatherings often become the backdrop for family traditions, the stuff memories are made of. Sitting together at the table sends a strong message: family comes first. It fosters a deep sense of belonging and love that can't be easily shaken.

These moments are more than just time spent together—they're investments in the heart and soul of your family. So, set the table, pull up a chair, and dive into these priceless moments. Trust me, they're worth every second.

Unplug to Connect

The only real way to connect with your family is to unplug—from the TV, texting, emails, notifications, and all the other distractions that pull us away from each other. Early in our marriage, we made a choice: the TV wouldn't rule our home. Even now, there's no TV in our living room, and for the first 25 years, we didn't have one in our master bedroom either. We figured if we wanted drama, we'd get it from real life, not reality TV! It's one of the best decisions we made to stay connected as a family.

But then the internet and smartphones came along—game-changers we didn't see coming. If we were raising kids today, we'd definitely set stricter boundaries. For now, we've boiled it down to one simple rule for the iPhone: no phones at the family dinner table or when eating out. And if one of us needs to remind the other, we say, "Put down your cigarettes," meaning you can indulge your nicotine later. It's our way of saying, if you want to keep up that habit, go to another room. But right now, be present with the person you love. This little nudge usually does the trick.

Create Family Traditions

The Jones home is built on traditions. We joke, 'Do something twice, and it's a tradition.' Quirky, but it's what holds us together.

One of our cherished traditions began when Jana and I first got married. On Christmas morning, we wanted the moment to be special for the family, not just a quick exchange of gifts. So, we created a tradition that we follow every year.

Our Christmas morning starts with Jana and me setting the table with the same dishes we use each year. Then, she makes pancakes shaped like Mickey Mouse ears. Before we eat breakfast, I read a prayer. After breakfast, we read the Christmas story from Luke Chapter 2 together, and everyone is assigned one of the characters from the story. As I read it, the family acts out their parts, making it a more interactive and engaging experience.

It's always fun to see who has to play the role of the donkey carrying Mary—there's usually some playful grumbling about that! Only after this do we gather under the Christmas tree and open gifts one at a time, very slowly. This creates a very meaningful and memorable time for our family. It's a special time, even as the grandkids are getting older.

just jana

Sometimes, we channel all our creativity into our careers but forget to bring that same ingenuity to our families. Yet, our families deserve our very best. That's why I make each grandkid a birthday cake. I'm not a baker, but for them, I become one. I personalize each cake, thinking about their interests and what they love, and I incorporate those elements into the cake. Each cake is a small way of showing them how much they mean to me.

Create a Fun Home

I am not sure "fun" is the right word. But for lack of a better word, let's go with it.

We want our home to be a place our kids and now grandkids love to be. This has been true for our kids growing up and their friends and now for our grandkids and sons-in-law. Today, we have a hot tub, swing set, beautiful deck, big yard, board games, a dedicated storage area for kids' toys, books, a cozy TV room, and "Mima's snack cabinet" with free food for the grandkids—and yet, I think my sons-in-law enjoy it more.

Both my sons-in-law are very good cooks. They put their heart into cooking fine meals. I don't cook at all.

Start with what you have. Our kids once turned the garage into a recording studio just for fun. With the grandkids, it is amazing how much chalk on the driveway creates amazing moments.

FINANCES: THE CONTENTMENT GAP

Perhaps the greatest culprit behind the gaps in our homes is discontentment. It makes us do some pretty crazy things—like buying stuff we don't need, with money we don't have, to impress people we don't even like. Sound familiar?

Finances are the window into your "contentment" gap. Want to know where your contentment truly lies? Just take a peek at your bank statements—it's all there in black and white. A lack of contentment is why managing money becomes one of the biggest sources of tension in marriage. Notice, I didn't say a lack of money is the source—it's a lack of contentment. Without contentment, all the money in the world won't satisfy your appetite for more.

When you cultivate genuine contentment and manage your finances wisely, it not only fills in the gaps of your marriage but also protects its edges and keeps the dirt out. On the flip side, poor money management doesn't just widen those gaps—it's like tossing a live grenade into your marriage. Spoiler alert: that never ends well.

Three Steps to a Great Financial Plan

Before diving into the steps, let's boil it down to one word: *Together.* Neither of you can say, "This isn't my strength, so I'll let the other person handle it." You must work together.

Dave Ramsey says in every relationship, there's a "nerd" and a "free spirit."[12] The nerd loves spreadsheets, budgets, and numbers. The free spirit, on the other hand, can't stand the thought of being boxed in by a budget. The trick is to blend these two color hues into a harmonious financial mosaic that works for both of you.

In our relationship, we can be both. I'm a nerd when it comes to holistic planning, but I'm a free spirit when it comes to everyday expenses. Jana is a nerd when it comes to daily expenses but a free spirit when it comes to grandkids.

1. Create Together

The first step is to create a financial plan together. The greatest way to fill in the gap of contentment is to create a spending plan based on percentages, not numbers.

When people say things like, "I don't make enough money," or "I can't save a lot of money," my response is simple: "Think percentages, not numbers." It's not about how much you make; it's about predetermining how you'll spend it by setting percentages that guide you and prevent discontentment.

Numbers will change over time. Percentages allow you to really moderate and manage your home finances. Percentages allow you to budget properly regardless of what you're making now or in the future.

Here's the base plan Jana and I use:

- 10% for giving
- 10% for savings/retirement (debt, emergency fund, etc.)

- 80% for living

I say base plan because, over the years, we've strengthened this. We've increased the percentage for giving and savings and decreased the percentage for living.

> **JJ just jana** *I was raised to pay cash for everything and pinch pennies like a pro. Troy wasn't bad at money; he just hadn't put much thought into it. Fun fact: When we were dating, Troy bounced a check he wrote me. I paid half for a suit for him, and the check bounced. Out of frustration, I asked Troy, "Are you in debt?" When he said yes . . . my heart skipped a beat. I couldn't believe a man of God had debt. It was modest college debt and needless to say, Troy and I had to figure out how to manage finances together.*

2. Keep Track Together

Over the years, Jana and I have been committed to keeping track of our finances together. Jana and I divide and conquer. She pays the bills, deposits funds, writes checks, and ensures all the details get done. I focus on the overall major expenses, percentages, savings, insurances, and retirement planning.

As you can imagine, the ways we've done this have drastically changed.

This may be hard for some to believe, but in the beginning of our marriage, Jana and I kept our budget in a spiral notebook. Picture us at the kitchen table, scribbling numbers and plans in those notebooks. We saved these notebooks as a record of our financial journey. There's something powerful about writing it down.

We also used the envelope system for a few years, where we allocated cash for different categories and put it in labeled envelopes. This method helped us stay disciplined and on track.

Whatever it takes, do it. Find a system that works for you and stick with it. It might seem old-fashioned, but these methods instilled discipline and kept us accountable, helping us place each financial tile precisely where it belongs.

Today, we use Quicken and other digital tools to manage our finances. While I'm in favor of these, I sometimes miss the old-fashioned way of carrying around those notebooks. Whatever you use, be committed to these tools. Adjust as needed, but don't just hope your finances will work out.

just jana JJ *When we first got married, we had very little money. We didn't have a fancy honeymoon, and we laugh now because we only spent $150 on my wedding ring—which I still wear to this day. We definitely didn't go out and buy brand-new furniture. We were modest in our spending across the board. Troy and I even shared one car for the first seven years of our marriage because we were determined to get out of debt. But let me tell you, we never felt 'broke.' We felt blessed. Being able to look back and see how far you've come is invaluable. Those days were fun. So if you're struggling to make ends meet, have some fun, create a plan, stop complaining about it, and move forward.*

3. Adjust and Tweak Together

A spending plan isn't a restrictive cage; it's a tool for freedom. It allows you to make informed decisions and avoid the stress of unexpected expenses. Remember, the spending plan is a living document. Adjust it as needed, but always make sure both of you are on the same page.

To adjust and tweak our plan, required us to have weekly meetings to discuss finances, especially in the first 10 years of our marriage. These meetings at first were about setting and agreeing on a spending plan. Now, they involve her paying bills and me updating Quicken to make sure everything lines up. As we do this, we talk and discuss financial details.

MVP: LET'S START GROUTING!

Strong marriages are intentional, not accidental. You don't just stumble into a healthy, thriving marriage any more than you accidentally run a marathon. It takes preparation, dedication, and yes—intentionality. Intentionality may not sound romantic; it's not the stuff of fairy tales or love songs, but let's face it—it's essential. Intentionality is what fills in the gap of your marriage mosaic, turning scattered pieces into a cohesive masterpiece.

Intent and being intentional are two entirely different things. You might have the intent to grow spiritually together, and that's a good start. But intent by itself is like a map without a destination—it's a nice idea, but it doesn't get you anywhere. If all it took was intent, everyone would be thriving in their marriage. But intent doesn't move the ball forward; intentionality does.

Think of it this way: Intent is deciding you want to score a touchdown. Intentionality is actually getting on the field, running the plays, and making sure you cross the goal line. Intent may inspire you, but intentionality is what drives you to action.

Intentionality means planning those date nights, even when you're exhausted. It's choosing to have the Safe and Secure conversations, even when you'd rather sweep things under the rug. It's showing up, day in and day out, making sure that your spouse knows they're seen, heard, and loved.

You'll either drift into a mundane marriage or intentionally create a masterpiece. And here's the truth: you naturally drift toward mundane, but you intentionally drift toward a masterpiece. What makes the difference? Intentionality.

So, talk about it. Talk about where you want to go as a couple, then make a plan to get there. Talk about what you want your future to look like, then take deliberate steps to make it happen.

Don't just hope for a great marriage—be intentional about building one.

Your MVP (Marriage Vision Plan)

I want you to intentionally develop a MVP (Marriage Vision Plan). A MVP answers two key questions: What is the vision for your marriage? And what's your plan to make this vision a reality?

Vision

I hope this book has sparked a vision for your marriage. Your marriage can be a masterpiece. You don't have to settle for a mundane, dry, or lifeless relationship.

Vision starts with this one question: who do you want to become as a couple? In other words, what are some things you want to accomplish together? What are the phrases and words that describe the kind of mosaic you want? These are powerful questions. They allow you to dive deep into your heart and discover what both of you truly want in your marriage.

Don't overcomplicate the word vision. It simply means "what you see." Vision is a clear picture of what you want the future to look like. It's your dream or goal, guiding you in the direction you want to go.

Start jotting down phrases and words that capture what you want your marriage to become. Every word and phrase makes up your vision.

NAPKIN EDITION #2

Next time you're out at a restaurant, grab a napkin and take a few minutes to jot down words or phrases that describe what you want your marriage to reflect. Don't overthink it—just start writing.

Once you're both done, share what you wrote. Sure, you might have to pause to give the server your order, but keep the conversation going. What stands out? Any differences? Common themes? Now, enjoy your dinner.

This isn't a one-and-done thing. Keep the conversation alive. After your napkin chat, text each other about the values that matter. Or better yet, plan a few days to get away and really dig in. Your marriage is worth the investment.

Eventually, you'll want to transfer this to a Google Doc or something. But for now, enjoy the process—because the process is way more important than the final product.

A marriage vision takes time. Sometimes you decide on it, and sometimes you find yourselves discovering your vision along the way.

For example, as newlyweds, we never had a vision to stay in one house for 30+ years, where our kids would be raised and our grandkids would create memories. We discovered it together as we went.

Jana and I were talking about our finances one day. As we planned, she spoke from her heart and said, "I'd rather leave the kids memories than money." That statement has become a cornerstone for us as a family.

Your vision evolves as your kids grow, life seasons change, personal goals shift, crisis hits, and you celebrate life's big moments.

Vision isn't something you can always sum up in one neat sentence—it's more like a piece of art than a math problem. But it's crucial. Start by jotting down words, phrases, and ideas that capture your marriage vision. Over time, try to distill it into one sentence if possible. Group these thoughts in a way that feels right to you.

Here are a few we use regularly.

- Faith: We passionately love God and serve His church together.
- Family: Our family loves each other deeply. Our grandkids are fully integrated into our traditions. Retreats and table moments are frequent. We create a legacy of "memories over money."
- Finances: Our vision is to live and give freely without being tied to work.
- Fitness: We stay fit and maintain optimal health for our age.
- Ministry: We'll look back on a career that truly made a difference in churches, pastors, and marriages.

So go ahead—dream a little. What dreams do you have together as a family?

Plan

How will you accomplish your vision? By making a plan. What rhythms do you need to create in your life to make this happen? What do you need to do daily, weekly, quarterly, and annually to make your marriage dream a reality?

A plan is a roadmap. It tells you how you'll do this.

I wish you could just say, "Hey Siri, take me to ________" and the plan would be mapped out for you. You know it's not that easy, or everyone would do it.

I love GPS. It gives you turn-by-turn directions on how to get to your destination. This involves mapping out the direct steps needed. What resources will you need? What obstacles might you encounter, and how will you overcome them?

This is where detailed planning and setting milestones come into play. Break down your dreams into actionable steps. If you want to buy a house, what does that look like financially? Decide when you will activate this plan. What is your starting day? When will you drive out of the driveway? Back to GPS.

I have a saying: "Dreams without deadlines are dead ends." What do I mean? Put dates and deadlines on your dream. Bite-size them into actionable items.

For example, at the age of 25, our vision was to live and give freely without being tied to work. This is significant. The intent was great, but the intentionality is what made the difference. We have worked our plan over 35 years, staying out of careless debt, putting specific percentages into retirement, and growing our giving to a specific percentage. This didn't happen overnight. It was intentional over 35 years.

One of our visions is for the family. Our family loves each other deeply. Our grandkids are fully integrated into our traditions. Retreats and table moments are frequent. We're creating a legacy of "memories over money." Here is our intentional approach: we have Papa Camp every summer with them. During Christmas, we do a Papa Express and decorate our house around the Polar Express theme. Jana bakes cakes for each of their birthdays. We take an annual vacation together with our grandkids. The vision must have a plan, or it's just a daydream.

just jana

Troy is very intentional about this. He is a gift to me. I have to work on this. I am not by nature a creator. But this is the beauty of our mosaic. He actually writes down the vision, I plan, and we do it together. It works well in our lives.

Do It

At the end of the day, it all boils down to this: "just do it." If I could follow you around for the next 24 hours, what would I see? Would I witness a couple living with intentionality, making deliberate choices that build up your marriage? Or would I see you getting lost in the weeds of life—distracted by the urgent instead of focusing on the important, missing out on what your marriage could truly become?

FILL IN THE GAPS

God is looking for you to fill in the gap for your spouse and home. In Ezekiel 22:30, He says, "I looked for someone among them who would build up the wall and stand before me in the gap on behalf of the land so I would not have to destroy it, but I found no one."

Gaps can sneak into your marriage and home life, whether you've been married for five minutes, five years, or fifty years. The enemy loves to slip in through those tiny cracks, aiming to shatter your mosaic piece by piece. These gaps start small—maybe a little neglect here, a tiny misunderstanding there—but they can quickly snowball into something much bigger.

So, will you stand with God? Will you stand with your spouse? Don't just sit back and let those gaps widen, threatening to destroy the masterpiece you're building together. Get bold. Get fed up with the little things that are trying to tear your marriage apart. Fill those gaps with fierce love, relentless prayer, and purposeful action. Don't let anything destroy the beauty of what God is creating in your marriage. Stand in the gap, fight for your spouse, and watch how God turns those fragile cracks into strong, unbreakable bonds.

ProTip for Men:

Seven Ways to fill in the gaps in your home.

Men, this is for you.

You make a difference in the home, whether you realize it or not. Some of you might feel a little intimidated by your role—but don't. Your presence, your support, and your leadership are pure gold. Here's how you can step up and lead well:

1. Love your wife fiercely.

   You want to be the best dad? Start by being the best husband. Your kids need to see you love their mom with passion, respect, and tenderness. Don't just talk about love—demonstrate it every day. Show them what it looks like to cherish a woman.

2. Set the tone.

   The atmosphere in your home? That's on you. You decide whether it's a place of peace or chaos. It's your job to bring calm, speak life, and create a space where everyone feels safe to grow and thrive.

3. Be present.

   Your job may be important, but not as important as being present at home. When you walk through that door, leave work behind. Be fully engaged with your wife and kids. Your presence means more than any paycheck ever will.

4. Serve first.

    True leadership isn't about being in charge—it's about serving first. Jesus modeled this perfectly by washing His disciples' feet. The strongest leaders at home are the ones willing to serve, sacrifice, and put their family's needs above their own.

5. Initiate family activities.

    Don't wait for someone else to make things happen. Take the lead. Plan the family dinners, vacations, and fun nights out. Show your family that they're your priority by making time for them.

6. Stay teachable.

    Here's the reality—you don't have all the answers. And that's okay. The moment you think you do, pride has already crept in. Stay humble, keep learning, and surround yourself with other men who can challenge you to grow.

7. Live with integrity.

    Your words are meaningless if your life doesn't back them up. Lead by example. If you want your kids to be honest, you be honest. If you want them to live with strong faith, live yours out loud. Remember, your life is the loudest sermon your family will ever hear.

So men, step up, lead with strength, and love with all you've got. Your family is counting on you.

COUPLES CHAT

MARRIAGE EDITION

1. On a scale of 1-10 (1 being low, 10 being high), how well do you think you and your spouse are doing at filling in the spiritual gaps? Home gap? Contentment gap? Intentionality gap? What are some small gaps you've noticed recently? How can you work together to fill these gaps before they grow larger?

2. How do you and your spouse differ in your approach to spirituality and faith? What steps can you take to respect and blend your unique ways of connecting with God?

3. What family traditions or rituals have been most meaningful in your marriage? How can you create new ones or strengthen existing ones to keep your family bond strong?

4. How do you handle financial decisions together? What adjustments can you make to ensure that both of you feel secure and content with your financial planning?

5. In what ways can you be more intentional in your marriage, particularly regarding your future goals and dreams? How can creating a Marriage Vision Plan (MVP) help you align your daily actions with your long-term vision?

6. When was the last time you had a "gap moment"—a time when something felt off in your marriage? How did you address it, and what can you learn from that experience to prevent future gaps?

7. How can you both be more intentional about standing in the gap for each other, especially during difficult times? What specific actions can you take to protect and strengthen your marriage?

ENGAGED EDITION

1. On a scale of 1-10 (1 being low, 10 being high), how well do you think you and your future spouse are doing at filling in the spiritual, home, contentment, and intentionality gaps? Are there any small gaps you've noticed in your relationship recently?

2. How do you and your future spouse differ in your approach to spirituality and faith? What steps can you take to respect and blend your unique ways of connecting with God?

3. What family traditions or rituals have been most meaningful to you as individuals? How can you create new traditions together?

4. How do you currently handle financial decisions as a couple? What adjustments or plans can you make to ensure that both of you feel secure, content, and aligned with your financial goals?

5. In what ways can you be more intentional in your relationship? How can developing a Marriage Vision Plan (MVP) help you align your daily actions with your long-term vision for your marriage?

6. Reflect on a time when something felt off in your relationship—a "gap moment." How did you address it, and what lessons can you take from that experience to prevent future gaps from widening in your marriage?

7. How can both of you be more intentional about standing in the gap for each other? What specific actions can you take to protect your relationship as you prepare for marriage?

5

POLISH YOUR MOSAIC

Make Love 

"NOT TONIGHT. I AM TIRED."

These few words are ones no woman wants to hear. Just kidding—I wanted to ensure you're reading closely.

Typically, these are the words a man fears the most. They're like a punch to the gut, a swift kick to the ego. It feels like rejection and leaves a man feeling unwanted.

Why is making love so sensitive for both men and women? Because in the bedroom, we're not just connecting physically—we're blending every color and hue of our marriage into a vivid masterpiece.

Imagine blending colors on a canvas. You might use a stiff brush, a rag, or a palette knife to forcefully mix the colors together. The pressure and speed of your strokes create bold, dynamic transitions, leaving visible brushstrokes and texture. This technique injects energy and movement into the artwork. It's vigorous, somewhat unpredictable, and results in a raw, textured blend.

In a real way, making love is like blending colors. No other act in marriage brings a couple together like this—not even close. It's a mosaic, where making love draws upon the three primary colors of your relationship, intertwines with the secondary colors, and reveals the unique shades that make your bond truly one-of-a-kind.

Understanding where the phrase "making love" comes from is helpful to adding texture to what it means to us today.

The phrase "making love" has a fascinating history. Originally, it had nothing to do with what we think of today. Back in the 16th and 17th centuries, "making love" was all about courting or wooing someone. Picture it—men and women engaging in flirtatious conversations, exchanging compliments, opening the door for each other, and doing everything they could to win the other person's affection. It was about romance, not sex.

Fast forward to the 20th century, and the meaning of "making love" started to change. As societal attitudes toward sex and relationships evolved, so did this phrase. By the mid-20th century, "making love" had become synonymous with sexual intimacy, especially when it involved deep affection and emotional connection between partners.

I'd like to go back to the 16th and 17th centuries and bring back their definition of making love. Making love was about caring, wooing, and winning each other's affection.

Think of it as the polish on a mosaic—making love brings out the colors, enhancing the beauty, and making everything shine in your marriage. Without sexual intimacy, your marriage will be dull and lifeless.

Polishing your mosaic means tending to the intimacy in your relationship. It's the act of refining, enhancing, and nurturing your connection. Without it, the vibrant colors of your marriage will fade.

Polishing ensures your mosaic remains a stunning masterpiece, reflecting the depth and beauty of your bond.

SEX IS A COVENANT RENEWAL

Before we polish your mosaic, let's back up for a moment and understand that God is the one who created sex. I was teaching on sexual intimacy to a married group when a close friend approached me, winked, and said, "Between the two of us, sex isn't that important if you are a Christian." His clear implication was that if you really know God and are spiritual, you don't need sex.

"NO!" I said to him, "Sex is a gift from God. It's a beautiful way to say I belong to you, forever."

Keller observes the first explicit mention of sex is in the famous passage of Genesis 2:24, quoted also by Paul in Ephesians 5, where male and female are united and become one flesh.[13] Before sin entered the world, Adam opened his eyes, saw Eve naked, and felt no shame. In fact, I imagine his first words were something like, "Wow, God, You've outdone Yourself!"

Keller provides a deep meaning for sexual intimacy: "Indeed, sex is perhaps the most powerful God-created way to help you give your entire self to another human being. Sex is God's appointed way for two people to reciprocally say to one another, "I belong completely, permanently, and exclusively to you."[14] You must not use sex to say anything less.

Marriage is about giving your entire self to your spouse. There's no other relationship on earth like it. Your spouse deserves exclusive rights to all of you—body, mind, and soul. Sexual intimacy is the sacred celebration of that covenant. For me, even the way I refer to Jana reflects this exclusivity. I call her my wife, my lover, my spouse—titles that are hers and hers alone.

There's a growing trend of calling your spouse your "best friend." But to me, that cheapens the significance of our covenant. I've got other "best friends," which is exactly why I don't use that term for our relationship. Jana's titles are reserved exclusively for her. She's the one I share a covenant love with—something far deeper than friendship. I won't diminish that by using a term that falls short of the depth of what we have.

Sex isn't just physical; it's deeply spiritual. It's a sacred covenant renewal. When you make love, you're not just sharing your bodies; you're intertwining your souls. Every time you make love, you are telling your spouse, "I belong completely, permanently, and exclusively to you." You're saying, "I choose you, over and over again."

Instead of hinting to your spouse about getting lucky tonight, let's start a new movement: "Tonight, let's go and renew our vows together." This vow renewal doesn't require a wedding dress, a best man, or a maid of honor. It's just the two of you!

JJ just jana

In the church, we're often guilty of preaching 'no sex until you're married.' We emphasize this before marriage, but then we fall silent after the wedding. No one wants to talk about it, and that's a grave mistake. The result? We let Netflix and YouTube define sexual intimacy for us. It's time we talk about it. Sex was created by God for a man and a woman to share something stunning and beautiful. It's where we literally become one flesh, where we renew our covenant vows frequently. It's where we say to our partner, 'I completely, permanently and exclusively belong to you.' The bedroom is where your marriage masterpiece should truly shine."

Four Ways to Polish Your Mosaic

Making love is the greatest act of intimacy you will ever have with someone. Intimacy is a word that means "into you I see." Sex is about letting your spouse see the real you. It's peeling back the layers and exposing your true self—your fears, dreams, and everything in between. In those moments of intimacy, you invite your partner to truly know you, and you say, "Here I am, without masks or walls."

This chapter is not just about having sex. It's about adding beautiful polish to your mosaic. It's about renewing the covenant vows to your spouse. So grab your polish, and let's add some sheen to your marriage as we renew our covenant vows to each other.

1. Understand Bedroom Communication

Most marriage books discuss how men and women communicate, but few tackle the unique dynamics of bedroom communication.

The bedroom is a sanctuary where you bond and connect deeply. In the bedroom, you blend the fiery red of sexual desire with the bright yellow of communication style, creating a mesmerizing orange sunset. Orange, the color of bonding and connection, beautifully represents this intimate space.

It represents deep soul connections and the contentment of being closely linked with your spouse.

Imagine the sunset at the end of the day, painting the sky in stunning hues of orange. It mirrors the landscape where earth meets nature, a reflection of perfect harmony and connection. This vibrant orange symbolizes the beautiful blending of your desires and communication, forming a bond as breathtaking and natural as a sunset.

To fully embrace this vibrant orange, dive headfirst into the fascinating differences in how men and women communicate in the bedroom.

I want to be careful not to stereotype. We all have different hues of red. However, understanding these overall unique nuances can transform your intimate life, making it richer and more connected.

Ladies, sex is heartfelt communication for a man. During sex, he hears that he completely, permanently, and exclusively belongs to you, or he hears, "I am not important to you." This isn't about men being shallow; it's about their need for physical touch to open their hearts. When making love, your man's heart is wide open, vulnerable, and eager for your nurturing touch.

Gentlemen, for a woman, sex is the result of heartfelt communication, not the shortcut to it. She wants to feel completely, permanently, and exclusively yours before she even thinks about opening up in the bedroom. So, if you're looking for a direct route, remember—you've got to touch her heart first. Think of it as the ultimate "pre-game warm-up" if you want her to give you her body.

What does this mean for a man? Slow down. Let me say it again . . . slow down. Sex starts when you speak the love language of your spouse. Turn on the music of tenderness and care for your wife. Become wildly curious about what this means for her. Engage in meaningful conversations, share your thoughts and feelings, and show her that you cherish her beyond physical attraction.

How about you, ladies? What does this practically mean? Prepare your heart before you enter the bedroom. Throughout the day, give yourself permission to start feeling romance toward your husband. You need to see the beautiful sunset in your bedroom. Many of you are missing this sunset because of the busyness and stress of life. Reflect on the moments of deep connection and let the warm glow of your love reignite the passion.

By taking the time to nurture your intimate bond, you can transform your bedroom into a sanctuary of vibrant orange, where love and desire blend seamlessly.

JJ just jana

We need to truly respect how men communicate in the bedroom. It's easy to dismiss this as shallow or think, "Is there a short circuit somewhere in his brain?" But the truth is, sex opens a man's heart. It's his way of communicating, with his emotions deeply involved. During sex, his red, yellow, blue, green, orange, and purple all come together in one moment. Think of it as a fireworks show and only you have the front-row seat. It's perhaps one of the greatest honors for a woman to witness these vibrant colors and hues come alive in a man. Look at it as it's your privilege to nurture these moments!

2. Treat Your Spouse Like Royalty

Making love is a beautiful fusion of our sexual desires (red) and emotions (yellow), creating the color purple . . . a realm of royalty and mystery in the bedroom. Purple brings depth and strength to your marriage, symbolizing a union that's powerful and profound.

In the bedroom, your spouse should feel like a king or queen. It's your moment to channel your inner Prince Charming or charming Cinderella—bringing grace, elegance, and a bit of playful humor to those intimate moments. After all, who wouldn't want to feel like royalty in the most private palace of all?

Treating your spouse like royalty involves a blend of respect, courtesy, and adherence to traditional protocols. Picture this: as you prepare for the evening, address each other with endearing titles. "I may not address Jana literally as "Your Majesty," or she doesn't address me as "King Troy" (though sometimes she calls me "Dr. Troy" when she's feeling flirty), but we do use terms that are personal and intimate in nature.

I am not necessarily suggesting you bow when your spouse walks into the bedroom, but they should feel this kind of royalty honor in your intimate moments. Being well-groomed, showing respect, and demonstrating deference only makes the purple shine brighter in the bedroom.

Whisper polite expressions into their ear, and show deep appreciation for their body. Compliment your queen or king, display humility and grace, and understand and respect any boundaries they may have.

By nurturing these moments with the elegance and poise of royalty, you'll keep the vibrant colors of your relationship shining bright.

Here are some practical ways to bring royalty to your bedroom:

- Set the scene with a clean, inviting space. Light candles, play soft music, and ensure the environment feels special.

- Show respect through your actions and words. Use affectionate titles, express gratitude, and make your spouse feel cherished and honored.

- Pay attention to your spouse's needs and desires. Ask what they enjoy and be willing to explore new ways to bring them pleasure.

- Express genuine appreciation for your spouse's body, mind, and spirit.

- Keep things exciting by introducing new experiences and surprises. Plan a special date night, try a new activity together, or bring a playful element into your intimate moments.

Ok, have some fun with this tonight. Grab a crown or a royal robe and add some majestic purple to your bedroom. Embrace the royal treatment and let your love reign supreme! Light some candles, play your favorite music, and create an atmosphere fit for royalty. Treat each other like the king and queen you are, and watch your connection deepen and your bond strengthen.

3. Develop Rhythm and Rhapsody

Here's the truth nobody wants to say—sex can become mundane. It takes intentionality and thoughtfulness to keep the spark alive in the bedroom.

You have to develop both rhythm and rhapsody. Those are two words you don't hear often when talking about making love. But they are essential.

At first glance, these two words seem to contradict each other. But they don't. Actually, they are both essential to make the passion in your bedroom shine brightly.

Rhythm | Show Up Frequently

How often should you make love? There's no one-size-fits-all answer to this. But here's the truth: it's probably more often than you think. Whatever your first response is, you might want to double it. The frequency of intimacy is a deeply personal decision, unique to every couple. To figure this out, you need to have safe and secure conversations about how often you're making love—no holding back.

Every couple must define what "frequent" means to them, and once you do, stick to it.

"Frequent" isn't just about how often something happens; it's about creating a rhythm that keeps your connection strong. My exercise trainer often tells me, "Be honest with your reps." He means be truthful about the number of repetitions you're doing during a workout—no cutting corners or exaggerating! As married couples, we need to be honest with our 'reps' too. Most couples think they're making love more often than they actually are. And as you might imagine, most men think it should be more frequent. Be honest with your reps. Honest as a couple.

Remember, making love is about so much more than just the physical act. It involves every aspect of who you are—your red, yellow, blue, and every other color on your marriage's color wheel. That's why it's crucial to define what "frequent" means for you as a couple.

JJ just jana *And here's a tip: Get a lock on your master bedroom door—especially when the kids are young. And a word of warning: skip the smart lock. Those kids might just hack the code and open it up from downstairs! Make it a golden rule in the house that if the door is locked, mom and dad need their privacy. Don't be afraid to communicate this. After all, you wouldn't want a little one barging in during your "top-secret meetings." Sure, the kids will eventually figure out what's going on behind those closed doors—probably during a therapy session when they're older—but at some level, that's okay.*

Why Define "Frequency"?

So, how often should you be intimate? This conversation shouldn't be a one-time thing. Check in with each other to make sure you're both on the same page and keeping things healthy. Here's a list of reasons why you and your spouse need to define "frequency":

1. Every Couple is Different: You need to discover the perfect balance—long enough to build anticipation and excitement, but short enough to prevent emotional distance. When you prioritize this, you're telling your spouse, "You matter. Our connection matters."

2. Life is Busy: Kids, work, church commitments—they all pile up. But here's the deal: you wouldn't skip meals because you're busy, right? Your intimate life is just as essential. It's not just a physical act; it's a profound expression of love, unity, and commitment.

3. Prompts Conversations: If the hue of red in your relationship feels off, it's a sign you need to talk. Many things can impact that red hue, and by discussing sexual intimacy, you keep the conversation alive between the two of you.

4. Protects from Temptation: Paul the apostle was crystal clear: Don't deprive each other except by mutual consent, and make sure it's for a short time. Why? So that Satan will not tempt you. Sexual frequency helps protect you both spiritually. I can already hear every man saying, "Preach it, pastor!"

As I mentioned in Chapter 2, there are several factors that can impact the different hues of red in your spouse. It's worth repeating here: past trauma, hormone levels, stress from work or finances, kids acting out, misunderstandings, unmet needs, or even the time of the month can all play a role.

Jana and I saw a psychologist while writing this book. And yes, you guessed it—sex came up. After three days of counseling, he looked at us very seriously and said, "Never, never, never forget this one thing." He paused . . . we leaned in . . . then he said with passion, "The three-day rule."

"What is this?" we asked.

He said out loud, "Never go beyond three days without making love." He even added that a little sanctified seduction wouldn't hurt either. We didn't have the guts to ask him what he meant by "sanctified seduction." I guess every couple will have to define that on their own. (I know some of you are already searching for his name and number—you might be more open to counseling now!)

For full transparency, Jana and I have had seasons where we didn't fully live up to this three-day rule. I suppose that's why we had to pay someone to tell us the obvious . . . While we've always talked openly about intimacy, life can sometimes get in the way. But we decided to be good clients and take our psychologist's advice. We agreed to the "three-day rule." Simply put, don't let more than three days pass without being intimate. This isn't about sticking to a rigid schedule; it's about maintaining a rhythm that keeps you and your spouse connected.

So, don't beat up your partner if the rhythm of making love isn't quite right. Instead, work together to find it. Have the conversation. Don't get legalistic—this is about making love, not clocking in at work. And as my physical trainer would say, "Be honest with your reps." Dont cheat each other. Keep it frequent.

just jana

It was a Sunday morning, and Troy and I were team teaching on Mother's Day. As we delved into the topic of the importance of moms, Troy was eloquently expounding on how to take care of the matriarchs of the home. As I listened, his list was long but all true. I'm not sure what came over me, but in a moment of candor, I blurted out, "Taking care of a lady is lots of work. . .I looked at Troy and said "All he needs is chicken and sex." To my surprise, the grandmas in the audience loved it the most. The entire church erupted in applause. I turned red as they laughed, almost giving me a standing ovation. Here's the truth about most men: they need food, you to show up naked, and praise when they do the small things. Don't underestimate the power of these words!

Rhapsody | Show up Enthusiastically!

Ok, rhapsody is not a word you see in every marriage book . . . heck, I am still working on pronouncing it. Jana is helping me by saying, "Think about it like Rap-So-D."

It's a powerful word. It's where both partners show up enthusiastically in the bedroom. Where both partners are passionate, expressive, and imaginative about their intimacy. Where both partners are committed to keeping it fresh and adding some creativity to your marital bedroom.

I am always surprised how we can be creative where we want to be. If a man loves his car, he will buy the newest toys, keep it clean, and be creative about its care. If a woman is into her career, she will go the extra mile and do everything she can to put energy into the career. We need to put this kind of creative energy and focus into the bedroom.

> **JJ just jana** *Ladies, this is where it's time to lean in and get creative. Treat your man like a king in the bedroom. Now, I'm not saying you need to literally call him 'King'—though, let's be honest, most men would love that—but show him respect, express honor, and let him celebrate his queen with energy and enthusiasm.*

During the seven-year wake-up call, we discovered some very helpful language to show up enthusiastically in the bedroom. Stay with me on this section. Some of this is descriptive in nature. However all three of these types of sex can add a rhapsody to your marriage that is beautiful.

Fast Food

Fast Food sex is quick, spontaneous, and often driven by urgency or the constraints of a busy life. It's the "we've got five minutes before the kids get home" kind of sex. It's about quickly having covenant renewal, saying, "I belong completely, permanently, and exclusively to you, but we need to make this quick."

It's easy to minimize fast food. Perhaps the metaphor by itself doesn't help. But in the context of marriage covenant, it can be deeply satisfying (and practical) because it fulfills a real need. Imagine you're driving home late, and you're starving. That fast-food drive-thru? It's a lifesaver. It's not gourmet, but it hits the spot. Fast Food sex serves a similar purpose. It's about connecting: quickly, intensely. Don't underestimate its value—it keeps the fire burning when life gets hectic.

Many times, we say a woman can get "hangry," meaning her hunger is turning into anger. Well, a man can get "hornstrated", meaning his hormones can turn into frustration (yes I just created a new word).

The goal is to enjoy fast food but not live on it. Back to my physical trainer . . . getting into the gym is half the battle. Sometimes you need to do a quick workout because of time and energy. However, many times the quick workout can turn into a full workout.

Home-Cooked

Home-Cooked sex is the comfort food of intimacy. It's deliberate, familiar, and nourishing. This is the "we have a free evening, let's make it special" kind of sex. It's about taking time to enjoy each other, savoring the moments, and reconnecting on a deeper level. Think of it as your favorite homemade meal. It's not rushed; it's prepared with love and attention.

Home-Cooked sex involves thoughtful touches, gentle caresses, and meaningful eye contact. It's the foundation of a healthy sexual relationship, offering warmth and stability. It's like coming home and smelling the pot roast, knowing that something wonderful and comforting is waiting for you. This type of intimacy is about being present with each other, creating a safe space where you can both relax and be yourselves. Just as a homemade meal is crafted with care, Home-Cooked sex is about investing time and effort into your relationship, ensuring it remains fulfilling and strong.

Gourmet

Gourmet sex is a luxurious, sensuous experience. It's planned, elaborate, and meant to be savored slowly. This is the "we're celebrating an anniversary, let's make it unforgettable" kind of sex. It's spending time renewing your covenant vows as a night to remember.

Picture a five-course meal at a fancy restaurant. The ambiance, the flavors, the presentation—it's all about creating a memorable experience. Gourmet sex involves setting the stage: candlelight, music, perhaps even a special outfit. It's about exploring new heights of pleasure and intimacy, making your partner feel adored and cherished.

One of the books we recommend to couples is called "101 Creative Nights of Sex." It has ideas for "him" and "her" each day. They are sealed up in the book. You tear it out, and only you know the idea. The ideas add spice and creativity to your bedroom. Now, for full disclosure, we are not approving of all the ideas. This is just one way to keep things fresh and creative in the bedroom.

> ## just jana
> ## JJ
>
> *Ladies, gourmet sex is like a fine dining experience—take your time and enjoy every moment. And remember, presentation matters. Look good for your man. Put on something sexy he likes to see. He may tear it off quickly. But it's for him and his enjoyment.*

4. Polish, Don't Poison Your Marriage Bed

Making love is a covenant renewal that says, "You belong to me completely, permanently, and exclusively." You are adding poison to your bedroom if you share this with anyone or anything else.

One of the greatest poisons to your marriage bed is pornography. It distorts the true meaning of intimacy and erodes trust and connection between you and your spouse. It's like inviting a rattlesnake into bed with you. Rattlesnakes are toxic, and their bites can cause severe damage and potentially be fatal if not treated promptly.

Your marriage bed needs polish, not poison. Interestingly, the literal substances of polish and poison can appear similar to the average eye, especially when they are in the form of clear or similarly colored liquids. They may appear similar, but one adds beauty and texture to your marriage, while the other brings death and destruction. Metaphorically speaking, the polish of making love will add beauty and texture to your mosaic. The poison of pornography will stifle and eventually destroy your marriage.

The writer of Hebrews expresses this beautifully: "Marriage should be honored by all, and the marriage bed kept pure, for God will judge the adulterer and all the sexually immoral" (Hebrews 13:4). Why does God despise adultery and sexual immorality? Because you can't say, "I completely, permanently, and exclusively belong to you" if you're saying it to someone or something else. Just ask anyone who has been impacted by adultery or sexual immorality—they'll tell you. It's painful, destructive, and has no place in the sacred bond of marriage.

One of our core values as a couple is that 100% of our sexual energy is directed toward each other and shared with no one else. Not even an innocent DM on Instagram or a private chat with an old fling on Facebook. 100% of your sexual energy needs to be directed towards each other. The only way to have a true connection is not to share an ounce of your sexual energy with anyone or anything else. The snake will bite every time.

To protect your bedroom from poison:

- Share your passwords with your spouse.

- Establish clear boundaries.

- Be transparent with each other about your interactions, especially online.

- Avoid situations where temptation might arise.

- Prioritize open communication and regularly discuss your commitment to keeping your marriage bed pure.

- Surround yourselves with other couples who share sexual purity.

- Don't allow a hint of sexual immorality in your life. Ephesians 5:3 should be our standard of sexual purity: "But among you, there must not be even a hint of sexual immorality."

WHEN THE RED ISN'T HOT

Don't freak out. It's normal.

After 35 years of marriage, let's get real—there are seasons when the red is blazing hot, and other times when it's like a soggy matchstick. This is reality, and it's all part of a beautiful mosaic. You can't expect fireworks 24/7. Sometimes, life hits hard, and intimacy takes a backseat.

A lot can cool down the temperature of your sex life—things like having a baby, hormone swings, stress, or chronic illnesses. For instance, after childbirth, doctors usually say, "Wait six weeks." And trust me, that can feel like an eternity. It's natural for these factors to turn down the heat, so it's important to be patient with each other during these times.

The key is for you and your spouse to figure out the issue and find a way forward—*together*. This is your mosaic. It might mean planning a getaway, consulting with a doctor, or even working with a counselor. It could also mean discovering new ways to spark romance. Don't just sit back and hope the temperature changes on its own; be proactive, intentional, and honest with each other.

Don't underestimate the power of simple acts—hugging, kissing, and holding hands. These aren't just nice gestures; they're the building blocks of intimacy that go far beyond the bedroom. It's not just about the physical; it's about the connection, the closeness, and the commitment. So, lean into these moments—they're just as vital in crafting your marriage masterpiece.

And hey, without getting too graphic, there's more than one way to light a fire. Sometimes, a quick, simple gesture of affection or touch can remind you both that you're still in this together. Other times, it's about creating space to build the mood and rekindle the flame. Embrace the variety—it's all part of keeping the mosaic vibrant.

HANDLE WITH CARE

Perhaps the greatest thing I can say about making love is this: handle with care. You have a one-of-a-kind gift you are sleeping with. Treat them like the treasure they are, something unique and irreplaceable, someone that no one else has. Your spouse is a masterpiece, a precious work of art crafted by God. Every touch, every kiss, every moment of intimacy should reflect the reverence and honor this masterpiece deserves. This isn't just about physical connection; it's about cherishing the whole person—heart, body, mind, and soul.

When you approach intimacy as a covenant renewal, you elevate it from a mere act to a profound expression of love and respect. Remember, your spouse's heart is in your hands. Handle it with the utmost care, tenderness, and devotion. Make every moment count, not just for the sake of your relationship, but to honor the divine gift that your marriage truly is.

Ok, stop reading this book and enjoy renewing your vows with your spouse tonight!

JJ
just jana

ProTip for Women:

Seven Ways to Romance Your Man.

1. Surprise him with his favorite meal.

    They say the way to a man's heart is through his stomach, and there's some truth to that. A homemade favorite can speak volumes.

2. Plan a spontaneous getaway.

    Whether it's a weekend escape or just a night away, a surprise getaway can reignite the spark and create lasting memories.

3. Leave love notes.

    Tuck sweet, simple notes in places he'll stumble upon—like his wallet, the bathroom mirror, or his car. These little surprises remind him of your love throughout the day.

4. Dress up for him.

    A little extra effort can go a long way. Wear something you know he loves, whether it's that dress he's always complimenting or something that makes you feel confident and sexy.

5. Plan a date night at home.

    Turn off the TV, put away the phones, and create a special evening just for the two of you. Whether it's cooking together,

enjoying a candlelit dinner, or talking by the fireplace, an intimate night at home can be just as romantic as a night out.

6. Offer secretive touches.

    Throughout the day, find playful moments to give him a little pat or place your hand on his leg while driving. It's a fun, flirty way to show affection.

7. Initiate intimacy.

    Don't wait for him to make the first move. Take the lead in the bedroom and show him that you desire him—confidence and passion go hand in hand.

COUPLES CHAT

MARRIAGE EDITION

1. On a scale of 1-10 (1 being low, 10 being high), how do you feel about your sexual intimacy currently? What does it mean to you to treat your spouse like royalty in the bedroom? How can you create an atmosphere where both of you feel cherished and valued?

2. How do you feel about the idea of making love as a covenant renewal ceremony? How can this perspective deepen your emotional and spiritual connection during intimate moments?

3. How do you and your spouse communicate your needs and desires in the bedroom? What can you do to improve your "bedroom communication" and ensure both of you feel heard and valued?

4. When was the last time you made intentional efforts to "polish" your marriage through intimate connection? How can you ensure that this important aspect of your relationship remains a priority?

5. How do you balance rhythm and rhapsody in your intimate life? What changes can you make to keep your physical connection both consistent and exciting?

6. How do you handle the potential "poisons" that could harm your marriage, like distractions or external temptations? What steps can you take to protect and strengthen the purity of your marriage bed?

7. In what ways can you and your spouse "handle with care" your unique marriage mosaic, especially when it comes to physical intimacy? How can you ensure that each encounter honors and cherishes the connection you share?

ENGAGED EDITION

1. On a scale of 1-10 (1 being low, 10 being high), is sexual intimacy a comfortable topic for you to discuss? How can you make this a safe, honest, and open conversation in your marriage without pointing fingers, ensuring that both of you feel heard and respected?

2. How do you feel about the idea of sexual intimacy as a way to renew your commitment and vows to each other? How can viewing intimacy in this way help you feel more connected emotionally and spiritually in marriage?

3. What does it mean to treat each other like royalty when it comes to intimacy? How can you create a space where both of you feel honored, cherished, and valued in your marriage?

4. How do you think you'll communicate your needs and desires when it comes to intimacy in marriage? What can you do now to ensure you have open and honest conversations about intimacy in a way that makes both of you feel valued?

5. What are some ways you can make sure that intimacy remains a priority in your future marriage? How do you balance life's busyness with keeping your connection strong?

6. How do you envision creating a balance between the frequency and excitement of intimacy in your marriage? What are some ways you can keep our physical connection fresh, fun, and meaningful?

7. How can you protect your relationship from distractions or temptations that could harm your future marriage? What steps can you take to safeguard your emotional and physical connection?

FINAL WORDS

LET'S FINISH STRONG! As we come to the end of this adventure together, my hope is that you've found both insight and inspiration as we've explored your Mosaic Marriage. God's desire is to take you and your spouse—two imperfect people—and turn you into a one-of-a-kind, stunning masterpiece.

But let's be real, this transformation isn't instant. It's not a quick fix or a one-time decision. It's built day by day, week by week, month by month, year by year, and yes, decade by decade. Every decision you make, each time you lean in, and even all the missteps, brings you closer to that masterpiece. The beauty is in the process—in the commitment to keep showing up and doing the work, even when it's hard.

There will be days when the pieces don't seem to fit, when the picture is unclear, and when you might feel like giving up. But remember, every masterpiece has moments of chaos before the beauty emerges. It's in those moments you have to trust the process, trust God's hand at work, and trust each other.

This journey isn't about perfection; it's about progress. It's about making the choice every day to love, forgive, grow, and move forward together. It's about embracing the challenges as opportunities to deepen your connection, strengthen your bond, and create something that truly reflects God's design for your marriage.

Along the way, as you create your mosaic:

- Clean your surface: Don't let bitterness and anger harden your heart.

- Discover your mosaic: Be wildly curious about your spouse.

- Set the tiles: Engage in safe and secure conversations.

- Fill the gaps: Do the finish work on your mosaic.

- Polish your mosaic: Make love. Renew your vows. Keep the spark alive.

But before we conclude, there's one final question you must consider:

At the end of the day, the strength and beauty of your marriage boil down to one simple question: who or what narrates your life? When I say "narrate," I mean who or what guides your decisions, gives your life meaning, and influences how you react to every situation? Who do you surrender to? Who makes the final call? Who really calls the shots?

Some of you might say, "No one narrates my life. I do." But by saying that, you've answered the question: You are the one who makes the final call.

For Jana and me, the One who narrates our lives is Jesus of Nazareth. He's not just the "secret sauce" of our mosaic; He is "The Sauce!" Our entire marriage is built on the Lordship of Christ and His Word. He is Lord. He is the one we surrender to. Every word we've shared in this book is rooted in our commitment to Christ as the Lord of our lives. He narrates, and He calls the shots.

Is Jesus the Lord of your life? Does He narrate every decision you make?

Some of you might consider yourselves Christians, but the truth is, Jesus isn't really Lord—you're still in charge. You haven't fully bent your knee at the cross.

Some of you might be prodigal sons or daughters. Maybe you've walked away from God, hurt by the church or simply drifting. This is your chance to come home. The Father is waiting with open arms.

And some of you might not be followers of Jesus at all. But I have good news—Jesus is calling you to Himself.

The Apostle Paul says in Romans 10:9: "If you declare with your mouth, 'Jesus is Lord,' and believe in your heart that God raised Him from the dead, you will be saved."

Yes, you can be saved. Paul gives us the answer to our salvation.

Today, I want to encourage you to do three things:

- A—Admit you are a sinner.

  Romans 3:23: "For all have sinned and fall short of the glory of God."

- B—Believe in Jesus alone.

  Romans 6:23: "For the wages of sin is death, but the gift of God is eternal life in Christ Jesus our Lord."

- C—Confess Him as LORD.

  Romans 10:9: "If you declare with your mouth, 'Jesus is Lord,' and believe in your heart that God raised him from the dead, you will be saved."

If you're ready to surrender to Jesus, I want to lead you in prayer. Right now, wherever you are, close your eyes and say this with me:

"Father God, today I admit I am a sinner. Forgive me. I put my faith and trust in Jesus alone. Today, I confess with my mouth Jesus is Lord, and I believe in my heart that God raised Him from the dead. Today, I am saved by the grace of God. I surrender everything I am to You. In Jesus' name! Amen."

If you just prayed this prayer, I celebrate with you today. All of heaven is rejoicing because you surrendered your life to Christ.

This is only the beginning. You are a child of God. Now, God wants you to follow Christ wholeheartedly.

I want to encourage you to do three things:

1. Find a community of faith.

2. Start digesting the Word of God. I encourage you to download the YouVersion app and develop a reading plan.

3. Get baptized in water. This is your way to go public with your faith.

JJ just jana

Father, thank You for every person who just surrendered their life to Christ. Heaven is throwing a party, and I'm celebrating with them! Welcome to the family of God! Touch them deeply, Lord, and breathe fresh life into their souls.

I'm also standing in the gap for every marriage represented here today and those about to be married. May each one be drenched in Your love and grace. I pray for a hedge of protection around every marriage, that they'll stand firm through every storm and come out stronger on the other side. Lord, let every marriage become the masterpiece You've designed it to be. In Jesus' mighty name, Amen.

COUPLES CHAT

MARRIAGE EDITION

1. On a scale of 1-10 (1 being low, 10 being high), how helpful has this book been for you and your spouse? What specific steps will you take to continue building your marriage masterpiece together?

2. Which aspect of creating your Mosaic Marriage—cleaning your surface, discovering your mosaic, setting the tiles, filling the gaps, or polishing your mosaic—do you feel needs the most attention right now? How can you both work on it together?

3. In what ways can you become more "wildly curious" about your spouse, as discussed in Chapter 2? How will this curiosity help you deepen your connection?

4. Safe and Secure conversations are essential to setting the tiles of your marriage mosaic. How do you plan to create an environment where both of you can speak openly and without fear of judgment?

5. What are some of the small gaps that have crept into your marriage over time? How can you actively work together to fill these gaps and protect your relationship from outside influences?

6. How do you plan to keep the spark alive in your marriage, ensuring that your mosaic remains vibrant and full of life? What does "polishing your mosaic" look like in your daily life?

7. Who or what narrates your life and marriage? How does this influence the decisions you make as a couple? If Jesus is the narrator of your lives, how do you keep Him at the center of your marriage?

ENGAGED EDITION

1. On a scale of 1-10 (1 being low, 10 being high), how helpful has this book been for you as a couple preparing for marriage? What specific steps do you plan to take as you begin building your marriage masterpiece together?

2. As you look forward to your marriage, which aspect of creating your Mosaic Marriage feels most important to focus on right now? How can you both work on it during your engagement to prepare for a strong foundation?

3. What are some ways you can become more "wildly curious" about each other, as discussed in Chapter 2? How will staying curious and learning more about each other help strengthen your connection as you prepare for marriage?

4. Safe and Secure conversations are key to building trust in your marriage. How do you plan to create an environment where both of you feel safe to express your thoughts and feelings openly, without fear of judgment, as you enter married life?

5. What small gaps or areas of misunderstanding do you think may develop as you start your marriage? How can you work together to proactively address these potential gaps and protect your relationship from challenges?

6. How do you plan to keep the excitement and intimacy alive in your marriage, ensuring that your relationship remains full of life and love?

7. Who or what will narrate your life and marriage as you begin this new chapter? How will this influence the decisions you make as a couple?

Research on Marriages

This research is taken from Feldhahn, Shaunti. The Good News About Marriage: Debunking Discouraging Myths about Marriage and Divorce (p. 102). Random House Publishing Group. Kindle Edition.

The Actual Divorce Rate

1. From the 1970s to today, many respected researchers have continued to believe in and refer to the 50 percent divorce rate, but this figure is always a projection based on assumptions about future trends.

2. The actual divorce rate is closer to 20 to 25 percent for first marriages and 31 percent for all marriages (including first and subsequent marriages).

3. Contrary to popular belief, the divorce rate has never approached 50 percent.

4. Today, 72 percent of people are still married to their first spouse. Among the 28 percent who aren't, some marriages ended in the death of a spouse, not divorce.

5. The divorce rate has been declining overall for years, with a significant decrease since its peak around 1980.

6. The most significant spike in divorces occurs not with the "seven-year itch," but with those who don't make it to their fifth anniversary.

7. The majority of remarriages last. Studies show that only 33 percent of second marriages end in divorce.

What Decreases the Divorce Rate

1. Divorce rate drops by 50 percent among churchgoers, primarily due to church attendance:

    Every study conducted has found that those who actively engage in their faith—by attending worship services, praying with their spouse, etc.—tend to be happier and closer in their marriages, with a significantly lower divorce rate.

2. Couples who marry in their mid-twenties or later have a much greater chance of making it to their twentieth anniversary.

3. College-educated individuals are more likely to marry later and stay committed to their marriages.

4. Research has found that 80 percent of couples who undergo counseling report that it helped save their marriage or significantly improved their relationship.

5. Data suggests that cohabiting couples are 33 percent more likely to divorce than those who wait until after marriage to live together.

Are Couples Happy?

1. Around 80 percent of marriages are happy, with about 30 percent being very happy.

2. The vast majority (93 percent or more) are glad they married their spouse and would do it all over again, including those who had once considered divorce.

3. In a vibrant church where couples are trying to put God first, more than half are not just "happy," but at the highest level of marital happiness and enjoyment.

4. Most marriage problems are not caused by major issues, and simple changes can make a big difference.

5. Research emphasizes that simply believing in the possibility of a successful marriage can significantly influence marital satisfaction and longevity.

6. Studies have discovered that small daily acts of kindness and appreciation are among the most powerful tools in sustaining a happy marriage.

APPENDIX B

Seven Steps to Repair a Broken Marriage

Marriage can sometimes feel like a beautiful mosaic shattered into pieces, scattered by the winds of bitterness, disappointments, and anger. When your marriage feels broken, it can seem overwhelming to know where to begin the healing process. But just as a mosaic artist carefully restores each tile to create a masterpiece, you too can start to mend your marriage. Here's how to begin:

1. Acknowledge the Brokenness

The first step to healing is admitting that there is a problem. Ignoring the issues or pretending they don't exist only allows them to fester and grow. Sit down with your spouse and openly acknowledge the bitterness, disappointments, and anger that have built up over time.

Joint Reflection:

- Share Feelings: Take turns sharing your feelings using "I" statements to express emotions without blaming your partner (e.g., "I feel hurt because . . ." or "I am disappointed when . . .").

- Understand Each Other: Listen to your spouse's feelings and validate their emotions, even if you don't fully agree.

2. Avoid the Blame Game

The instinct to blame your spouse for the problems in your marriage can be strong, but it only deepens the divide. Instead of pointing fingers, approach the situation with a team mentality—both of you working together to repair the relationship.

Action Steps:

- Reflect Together: Discuss the challenges without assigning blame. Focus on the "we" instead of "you."
- Team Mentality: Remind yourselves that you are in this together, working toward the common goal of repairing the marriage.

3. Seek Forgiveness and Offer Forgiveness

Bitterness and anger often stem from unresolved hurt. Forgiveness is not about excusing the wrongs done to you but about freeing yourself from the burden of carrying that pain.

Steps to Forgiveness:

- Apologize Sincerely: If you have wronged your spouse, apologize sincerely. Acknowledge your actions and express genuine remorse.
- Forgive Your Spouse: Release the bitterness you hold against your spouse. This might not happen overnight, but commit to the journey of forgiveness.

- Forgiveness Journal: Write down your grievances and then, one by one, write a statement of forgiveness for each. Share this with your spouse in a calm and loving manner.

4. Rebuild Trust Through Honest Communication

Trust is the foundation of a healthy marriage. When it's broken, it takes time and effort to rebuild. Start by creating a safe space for honest, open communication.

Strategies:

- Regular Check-Ins: Set aside time each week to discuss your feelings and the state of your marriage. Make this a priority.
- Active Listening: Listen to your spouse without interrupting. Validate their feelings, even if you disagree with their perspective.
- Communication Workshop: Attend a communication workshop or read books together on effective communication in marriage.

5. Address Unmet Expectations

Unmet expectations can lead to disappointment and resentment. It's crucial to discuss and realign your expectations with your spouse.

Steps to Address Expectations:

- Identify Expectations: Discuss what each of you expects from the marriage and from each other.
- Realistic Adjustments: Realign your expectations to be more realistic and achievable.

- Expectation Worksheet: Write down your expectations in various areas (e.g., household responsibilities, emotional support, financial management) and discuss how you can meet each other halfway.

6. Commit to Change and Growth

Healing a broken marriage requires commitment from both partners. You must be willing to put in the work to grow individually and as a couple.

Steps to Commitment:

- Personal Growth: Commit to personal growth through self-reflection, reading, and possibly individual and / or couple's therapy.
- Couple's Growth: Engage in activities that strengthen your bond, such as date nights, hobbies, and spiritual practices.:
- Growth Plan: Create a plan with specific goals for both personal and couple's growth. Review and adjust this plan regularly.

7. Seek Professional Help

Sometimes, the wounds are too deep to heal on your own. Seeking the help of a professional counselor can provide the guidance and tools needed to mend your marriage.

Options:

- Marriage Counseling: A licensed therapist can help you navigate through your issues and develop healthy coping mechanisms.
- Support Groups: Join a support group of Bible study for couples to share experiences and gain insights from others facing similar challenges.

8. Rediscover Joy and Intimacy

Bitterness and anger can erode the joy and intimacy in your marriage. Work on rediscovering what made you fall in love in the first place.

Activities to Rediscover Joy:

- Date Nights: Regularly schedule date nights to reconnect and enjoy each other's company.
- Shared Interests: Engage in activities that you both enjoy and that bring you closer together.
- Memory Lane: Spend an evening reminiscing about your favorite memories together. Look at old photos, watch your wedding video, and talk about the happy times.

APPENDIX C

*5 Intentional Conversations for Couples
Before and After Marriage*

1. Sexual Intimacy

   - How often do we want to be intimate?

   - What types of intimacy do we prefer?

   - What are our emotional and physical needs?

   - How do we prioritize intimacy?

2. Finances

   - How do we work together in our finances?

   - How should we budget and manage our spending habits?

   - How much should we save and invest each month?

   - How will we handle and pay off any debts we have?

   - What are our financial goals for the short-term and long-term?

3. Parenting

   - Do we want to have children? If so, how many and when?

   - What are our parenting styles and approaches to discipline?

- How do we agree (blend) our differing styles—and who might we involve if that becomes an issue?
- How much should extended family be involved in child-rearing?

4. Religious and Spiritual Beliefs
   - What are our personal beliefs and practices?
   - How involved do we want to be in church life?
   - Are we in agreement with each other's ministry involvement(s)?
   - How will our beliefs impact our family life and raising children?

5. Life Goals and Dreams
   - What are our personal and professional ambitions?
   - What travel and adventure plans do we have?
   - Do we prefer city, suburb, or rural living?
   - Do we want to own a home or rent?
   - Should we move to a different home?
   - Should we downsize?

NOTES

Open

1 Steve Perry, Neal Schon, Jonathan Cain, "Don't Stop Believin'," Escape, Columbia Records, 1981.

2 Feldhahn, Shaunti. *The Good News About Marriage* (p. 2). Random House Publishing Group. Kindle Edition.

3 Keller, Timothy; Keller, Kathy. *The Meaning of Marriage* (p. 223). Penguin Publishing Group. Kindle Edition.

Chapter 1

4 The Billy Graham Library. "Remembering Ruth Bell Graham," *The Archive Collection* July 1, 2013 https://billygrahamlibrary.org/remembering-ruth-bell-graham-2/

5 Keller, Timothy; Keller, Kathy. *The Meaning of Marriage* (p. 65). Penguin Publishing Group. Kindle Edition.

6 Keller, Timothy; Keller, Kathy. *The Meaning of Marriage* (p. 65). Penguin Publishing Group. Kindle Edition.

7 "Deferring." Merriam-Webster.com. *Merriam-Webster, Inc.* 2025. include URL

8   Kominsky, Selma, "Billy & Ruth Graham: Couple of Purity," *Marked Ministry Online Magazine*, June 2, 2017. https://markedministry. com/2017/06/02/billy-ruth-graham-couple-of-purity/

Chapter 2

9   "Lionize." Dictionary.com. *Dictionary.com, LLC.* 2025. https://www. dictionary.com/browse/lionize

Chapter 4

10   Feldhahn, Shaunti. *The Good News About Marriage* (p. 69). Random House Publishing Group. Kindle Edition.

11   Feldhahn, Shaunti. *The Good News About Marriage* (p. 69). Random House Publishing Group. Kindle Edition.

12   Ramsey Solutions. "Nerds and Free Spirits Can Unite Over the Budget." *Ramsey*, August 26, 2021. https://www.ramseysolutions.com/ budgeting/nerds-and-free-spirits-can-unite-over-the-budget?srslti-d=AfmBOooYbZsXVX1tpauML7jCehQ2DYX2v7iqDlB3nTySaf-PVDhG2zFML.

Chapter 5

13   Keller, Timothy; Keller, Kathy. *The Meaning of Marriage* (p. 222). Penguin Publishing Group. Kindle Edition.

14   Keller, Timothy; Keller, Kathy. *The Meaning of Marriage* (pp. 223-224). Penguin Publishing Group. Kindle Edition.

To request Troy and Jana to speak at your marriage event
or conference, contact them at drtroyjones.com